The Vote Motive

The Vote Motive

GORDON TULLOCK

EDITED AND WITH AN INTRODUCTION BY
PETER KURRILD-KLITGAARD

WITH COMMENTARIES BY
CHARLES K. ROWLEY
STEFAN VOIGT
MICHAEL C. MUNGER

The Institute of Economic Affairs

The Vote Motive first published as Hobart Paperback 9 in 1976 by
The Institute of Economic Affairs

This revised edition with commentaries first published in Great Britain in 2006 by
The Institute of Economic Affairs
2 Lord North Street
Westminster
London sw1p 3lb
in association with Profile Books Ltd

The mission of the Institute of Economic Affairs is to improve public understanding of the fundamental institutions of a free society, by analysing and expounding the role of markets in solving economic and social problems.

A CIP catalogue record for this book is available from the British Library.

ISBN-10: 0 255 36577 2
ISBN-13: 978 0 255 36577 2

Many IEA publications are translated into languages other than English or are reprinted. Permission to translate or to reprint should be sought from the Director General at the address above.

Typeset in Stone by MacGuru Ltd
info@macguru.org.uk

Printed and bound in Great Britain by Hobbs the Printers

CONTENTS

THE AUTHORS

Peter Kurrild-Klitgaard was born in 1966. He is Professor of Political Theory and Comparative Politics in the Department of Political Science, University of Copenhagen. He has a PhD (Political Science) and an MSc and a BA from the University of Copenhagen, and an MA from Columbia University. He is European editor of the journal *Public Choice*.

Michael C. Munger was born in 1959. He is Professor in the Department of Political Science and Department of Economics at Duke University. He has a PhD and an MA (Economics) from Washington University, and a BA from Davidson College. He is North American editor of the journal *Public Choice* and former president of the Public Choice Society.

Charles K. Rowley was born in 1939. He is Duncan Black Professor of Economics in the Department of Economics, George Mason University, and General Director of the Locke Institute. He has a PhD and a BA (Economics) from the University of Nottingham. He is editor of *The Selected Works of Gordon Tullock*, editor of the journal *Public Choice* and former president of the European Public Choice Society.

Gordon Tullock is University Professor of Law and Economics and Distinguished Research Fellow at the James M. Buchanan Center for Political Economy at George Mason University. He holds a joint teaching position in the Department of Economics and the School of Law. Professor Tullock is the author of 23 books, including *Calculus of Consent* (1962) (with Professor James M. Buchanan), *The Politics of Bureaucracy*

(1965), *Private Wants, Public Means* (1970), *The Logic of the Law* (1971), *Autocracy* (1987), *Rent-Seeking* (1993), *The Economics of Non-Human Societies* (1994) and *On Voting: A Public Choice Approach* (1998). He has also written several hundred papers on economics, public choice, law and economics, bio-economics and foreign affairs. In 1966, Professor Tullock became the founding editor of *Papers in Non-Market Decision-Making*, which was later renamed *Public Choice*. He remained senior editor of *Public Choice* until May 1990. He has also served as president of the Public Choice Society, the Southern Economic Association and the Western Economic Association. In 1996 he was elected to the *American Political Science Review* Hall of Fame, and in 1998 he was recognised as a Distinguished Fellow of the American Economic Association.

Stefan Voigt was born in 1962. He is Professor of Economic Policy in the Department of Economic Policy, University of Kassel, and in the International Centre for Economic Research (ICER), Turin. He is a member of the editorial board of the journal *Public Choice* and associate editor of the *Review of Austrian Economics*.

FOREWORD

Most people generally accept that individuals' actions in a market economy are motivated by self-interest. Remarkably, many intellectuals who deride market processes and who are highly critical of the motivation for individuals' actions within a market call for government intervention without considering for a moment whether the forces that motivate the actions of voters, bureaucrats and politicians are also based on self-interest.

It is, of course, true that public-spirited individuals may take into account a range of issues when voting on, enacting or administering government policy. But is it not wise to assume that self-interest is important? Certainly when one observes political protests in France, lobbying to keep hospital services open in the UK and the actions of the political establishment within the European Union, it is quite clear that self-interest plays a major role in the political process. French farmers campaign for the continuation of a system of subsidies and import restrictions in the name of 'solidarity', while those who lose from such policies are some of the poorest people in the world. At the present time, there are campaigns in a number of towns in England against ward closures in local hospitals: rarely are voters in a locality willing to accept such closures, even if they lead to better-resourced services over the region as a whole.

The pursuit of self-interest is, of course, dangerous in the political process while generally being beneficial in markets. Transactions can take place within a market only by mutual agreement, and any transactions must be in the interests of both parties. In the political process there are few constraints on the exercise of self-interest, except for an election every four or five years. It is therefore important to discover how self-interest might affect the behaviour of voters, bureaucrats and politicians, and how it might affect policy outcomes.

Public choice economics is thus crucial in understanding the damaging role that government can play in economic life. The market may not lead to perfect outcomes but there is no such concept as a disinterested, omniscient government that can perfect the imperfections.

In many respects the role of government has expanded in both the USA and the UK since the publication of the first edition of *The Vote Motive* in 1976. There are however signs that politicians, and even regulators, are more aware of the limitations that governmental bodies face when trying to improve upon market outcomes than was the case in 1976. There is no question that the work of Gordon Tullock and others, popularised by the IEA, has made a considerable impact, but, as public choice economics tells us, the nature of the political process is such that battle must continue to make sure that the public are aware of the fact that the vote motive is as important in public life as the profit motive is in commercial life. It is for this reason that the IEA is delighted to publish this second edition of *The Vote Motive* with commentaries from a number of experts in the field of public choice economics.

The views expressed in Hobart Paperback 33 are, as in all IEA publications, those of the authors and not those of the Institute (which has no corporate view), its managing trustees, Academic Advisory Council members or senior staff.

PHILIP BOOTH
Editorial and Programme Director,
Institute of Economic Affairs
Professor of Insurance and Risk Management,
Sir John Cass Business School, City University
November 2006

SUMMARY

- Public choice theory applies the techniques of economic analysis (monopoly, competition, information costs, etc.) to political and bureaucratic behaviour.

- It drops the conventional assumption that politicians and bureaucrats try to serve only 'the public interest' and more realistically assumes that, as elsewhere, they try to serve their own interests by, for example, re-election and empire-building. The vote motive in politics is the profit motive in industry.

- It analyses techniques ('constraints') in the structure of government to make self-interest more nearly coincide with the public interest, as in a competitive market.

- A main conclusion is that decentralised is more efficient than centralised government. A second is that simple majorities are less efficient than 'reinforced majorities' (for example, two-thirds) for some legislation.

- In two-party systems the parties tend to approach a consensus; in three- (or more) party systems they seem to diverge but the resulting coalition approaches a similar consensus; and the wings tend to form separate parties.

- Logrolling, the exchange of undertakings to support others' favoured policies, is usually concealed but dominates the selection of policy in representative government. It shapes party manifestos, coalitions and policies.

- In bureaucracies self-interest would tend to coincide with the public interest if, as in industry, they disclosed more information and were subject to competition from other bureaucracies and private producers.

- These reforms in the structure of government should be tried in small-scale experimentation.
- Public choice theory, by elucidating the pressure of trade unions on government, is better than pure monetary theory or cost-push theory in explaining inflation.
- Public choice theory has, since 1960, been revealing the strengths and 'imperfections' of government as established economic theory since 1776 has revealed the strength and 'imperfections' of the market. It thus provides a rational explanation for economically irrational policies such as on agricultural subsidies, commuter fares, education, health services and trade barriers.

EDITOR'S INTRODUCTION
Peter Kurrild-Klitgaard, University of Copenhagen

It is almost a truism to state that this or that book 'changed my life' or to claim boldly that it is 'one of the most important books of our times'. In the case of *The Vote Motive* (Tullock, 1976a), I can certainly testify that the first is true at a very personal level – and that I am also convinced that the book, as slim as it is, in fact has had significance that is larger than most people would think.

When *The Vote Motive* was originally published by the Institute of Economic Affairs in 1976, the field that was to be widely known as 'public choice theory' was still only on the verge of its big intellectual breakthrough. Over the previous twenty years this research field – the application of economic reasoning to the study of political phenomena – had rapidly developed as one of the most innovative and fascinating strands within modern social scientific thinking, but it was not yet quite a movement and it had not yet had the big impact on political analysis, political discourse and decision-making that it was to have within the next decade.

Also, *The Vote Motive*'s role does not lie in being one of the 'big' books of the public choice tradition, such as Anthony Downs' *An Economic Theory of Democracy* (Downs, 1957), Duncan Black's *The Theory of Committees and Elections* (Black, 1958), Tullock's grand collaboration with James M. Buchanan, *The Calculus of Consent* (Buchanan and Tullock, 1962), William H. Riker's *The Theory of Political Coalitions* (Riker, 1962) or Mancur Olson's *The Logic of Collective Action* (Olson, 1965). It does not represent a major, new contribution as these did in each of their different ways. As Tullock notes in his new introduction to this 2006 edition of the monograph, 'It was an effort to introduce the methodology of economics to politics. ... Missionary activity in a new field is always helpful for the progress of science. This easy-to-read introduction should be a big help in such activity.'

And indeed it was – and is. In fact, *The Vote Motive* was in more ways than one an 'intermediary' publication – it came at a time when the tide was changing and its primary function was practical. The book's importance lies in the fact that it was perhaps the first non-technical presentation of public choice analysis and in that it was directed more towards students, journalists and political decision-makers than to the relatively narrow circles of economists, political scientists, legal scholars and sociologists already familiar with the approach.

This was no accident. The Institute of Economic Affairs was even before the 1970s at the forefront of applying ideas such as those embodied in the public choice analysis to the formulation of specific proposals for political reform, and the book represented a conscious attempt to get wider recognition of public choice analysis than the more technical works in books and academic journals. John Blundell and Colin Robinson of the IEA have – in a contribution to an online Festschrift in honour of Tullock – neatly summarised the situation and the reasoning:

> [In Britain during the 1970s] most economists still assumed that government is the impartial servant of the public good and that the public good is capable of definition. The research agenda in public choice which by then was being established in the United States did not exist in Britain.
>
> After seeing and publishing *The Vote Motive*, it took Ralph Harris and Arthur Seldon very little time to recognise the significance of this new way of analysing government action. They realised that it undermined the market failure approach to government policy-making, which relied on the assumption that benevolent and far-sighted governments could be relied on to clear up the failings of private markets. After *The Vote Motive*, people in government could no longer reasonably be regarded as different from those in the private sector: government 'servants' could most likely be assumed to be pursuing their own interests, much

like private market participants, though not with such benign effects because of the monopoly power of government. For a host of reasons, government action would fail and would have results different from those intended. (Blundell and Robinson, 2002: 1)

In fact, the publication of the book led the IEA to organise a conference on 'The Economics of Politics' in 1978, which again resulted in a widely read book by that name (Buchanan, 1978). Because of *The Vote Motive*'s effectiveness at introducing public choice analysis, the book was soon translated into several languages, at least a dozen according to one count and including French (1978), Spanish (1979), Swedish (1982, with two later editions, each one longer than the previous), Italian (1984) and Korean (1994). Furthermore, owing to its accessible nature major parts of the presentation made their way into other texts that needed to present the basics of the new theory of how self-interest drives the political process (for example, the Danish book by Pedersen and Petersen, 1980).

In this way many European academics, journalists and people active in politics had their very first introduction to public choice analysis from *The Vote Motive*. After all, European universities of the 1970s and 1980s were not exactly places that offered much scope for courses and research in such a politically incorrect line of thought based on methodological individualism, a modelling of actors as being rational utility-maximisers and the exchange paradigm, and as such there was a useful place for an easy-to-read summary of this whole line of thought. In my own case, it happened in 1985, when I was a first-year student of political science and was confronted with reading lists that had everything about any variety of Marxist thought – from 'capital logic' to the Frankfurt School – and little else. Indeed, the most 'bourgeois' theories we were presented with were the American 'pluralist' tradition represented by Robert Dahl (for example, Dahl, 1956), whose idyllic – almost naive – portrayal of the political process was part of what the public choice theorists had reacted against. But a good friend of mine, who was a student of economics, recommended that I read some public choice theory, and from a mutual friend I obtained a copy of the Swedish edition of *The Vote Motive*, published by the free-market think-tank Timbro (Tullock, 1976b). For my part the rest is – as they say – history.

It is also more than a good guess that the authors of the hugely successful (and hence, in a sense, influential) British 1980s TV series *Yes Minister* and *Yes Prime Minister* may have gained at least part of their obvious familiarity with public choice analysis of the behaviour of politicians, bureaucrats and interest groups from having read the IEA's little monograph.[1]

Owing to the publications of such think tanks as the IEA and Timbro many of the theoretical insights developed by public choice analysis also made their way into practical political proposals. For example, such ideas as privatisation, vouchers, deregulation and limits on taxes and spending, etc., characteristic of many political initiatives over the last 30 years, are almost all ultimately inspired by the ideas of public choice theorists channelled through the work of think tanks into the domain of actual political decision-making. The reader may take the IEA's word for that:

> ... Gordon's ideas in *The Vote Motive* ... supplied a much-needed source of inspiration for IEA authors. The Institute's papers had, from the beginning, challenged the idea that government action can always improve on the outcome of a market. But, until *The Vote Motive* came along, IEA authors lacked a clear intellectual basis for their challenges. Gordon's work provided them with that intellectual basis, liberating them from the constraints of mainstream economics. Since *The Vote Motive*, the ideas of the public choice school have permeated IEA papers to such an extent that virtually all of them have those ideas at their core. (Blundell and Robinson, 2002: 2)

---

1   On the public choice inspiration for the show, see, for example, Borins, 1988. Sir Anthony Jay, one of the show's authors (the other being Jonathan Lynn), has on several occasions acknowledged his debt to public choice analysis and the IEA (for example, Jay, 2001).

As such the true impact of works like *The Vote Motive* may be much, much greater than is apparent at first sight, and it is therefore quite appropriate that the IEA now publishes a 30-year anniversary edition. Part One of this monograph begins with a new introduction to *The Vote Motive* by Gordon Tullock. This is followed by a reprint of the original text. Part Two comprises contributions from three of the world's leading public choice scholars. These writers, all closely associated with the journal *Public Choice*, founded by Tullock, critically assess and lend a perspective to *The Vote Motive*. Charles K. Rowley is a British-born but USA-based economist, who for many years has been the journal's editor and recently edited *The Selected Works of Gordon Tullock* for Liberty Fund; Stefan Voigt is a German economist at the forefront of the development and application of that sub-field of public choice known as 'constitutional political economy'; and Michael Munger is an American economist, who is among the leading scholars of public choice within US political science. By giving their own unique perspectives, they together pay a fitting tribute to one of the truly great and inspiring scholars of politics of the twentieth century.

References

Black, D. ([1958] 1998), *The Theory of Committees and Elections*, 2nd review edn, ed. R. A. Newing, I. McLean, A. McMilland and B. L. Monroe, Dordrecht: Kluwer Academic Publishers.

Blundell, J., and C. Robinson (2002), 'Gordon Tullock and the IEA: bridging the Atlantic Institute of Economic Affairs', http://publicchoice.info/TullockTales/JBlundellt.pdf.

Borins, S. F. (1988), 'Public choice: "Yes Minister" made it popular, but does winning the Nobel Prize make it true?', *Canadian Public Administration*, 31(1).

Buchanan, J. M. (1978), *The Economics of Politics*, London: Institute of Economic Affairs.

Buchanan, J. M., and G. Tullock ([1962] 2004), *The Calculus of Consent: Logical Foundations of Constitutional Democracy*, vol. 2 of *The Selected Works of Gordon Tullock*, ed. C. K. Rowley, Indianapolis, IN: Liberty Fund.

Dahl, R. A. (1956), *A Preface to Democratic Theory*, New Haven, CT: Yale University Press.

Downs, A. (1957), *An Economic Theory of Democracy*, New York: Harper & Row.

Jay, A. (2001), 'Yes Minister, and the IEA', in R. Harris and A. Seldon (eds), *A Conversation with Harris and Seldon*, London: Institute of Economic Affairs, pp. 77–80.

Olson, M. ([1965] 1971), *The Logic of Collective Action: Public Goods and the Theory of Groups*, Cambridge: Harvard University Press.

Pedersen, K. M., and J. H. Petersen (1980), *Hvorfor Kan den Offentlige Sektor ikke Styres? Økonomisk Politik – Politisk Økonomi*, Copenhagen: Berlingske Forlag.

Riker, W. H. (1962), *The Theory of Political Coalitions*, New Haven, CT: Yale University Press.

Tullock, G. (1976a), *The Vote Motive*, Hobart Paperback 9, London: Institute of Economic Affairs.

Tullock, G. ([1976b] 1982), *Den Politiska Marknaden: En Introduktion Till Public Choice-Skolan*, Stockholm: Timbro.

The Vote Motive

Part 1

THE VOTE MOTIVE

INTRODUCTION
Gordon Tullock

It is now 30 years since the IEA first published *The Vote Motive*. They also reprinted it 28 years ago. At that time public choice was still a new field of study. Many economists and political scientists had never heard of it. This small booklet probably introduced many people to the subject. I hope that it was only an introduction. It inspired many scholars to continue their study in the field.

As was usual for IEA books at that time, Arthur Seldon did a spectacularly good job of editing. Indeed, he could almost be called co-author. He also arranged for Professor Perlman to produce a commentary which was no doubt of great use to English readers. Since Seldon did the same superb job of editing and practically rewriting many other IEA publications, he can claim to be a major influence in the improvement of economics and political science not only in England but also in the remainder of the English-speaking world. My memory of his work makes me regret that the reader of this note will get Tullock in pure form rather than a drastically improved version benefiting from Seldon's work.

The subject was revolutionary at the time it was published. That is not because people had not thought about political problems in democracies or were firmly convinced by their high school civics course that the subject was in essence a branch of ethics. By the dominant myth, the voters selected the best men to represent them, and those representatives then selected the best course of action for the government.

Oddly this general view was combined with a general, and well-merited, distrust of politicians. They were thought to be tricky, and lacking in serious scruples. Nevertheless, democracy was thought to be the best way of running government, mainly because the others were so bad.

Today almost half of the human race lives in democratic states. This is a record since that proportion was never before achieved. If we look at the world, however, the record is only a small source of satisfaction. The most rapidly growing large country, China, is emphatically not a democracy. There is also some doubt as to whether Russia will remain a democracy: its current president is showing signs of becoming a dictator.

There's also the problem of India. India measured by population is, by a wide margin, the largest democracy. Questions as to whether it is, or will remain, a democracy are sensible. From the time that the British withdrew the prime minister was always a member of the same family until the last male adult of that family was assassinated. This left the leadership of that family in the hands of a woman who had the further handicap of being an Italian. She decided not to contest the prime ministership and it fell into the hands of an opposing party.

Looking at this from the standpoint of my own view on policy, the change was wise. The Congress Party had managed the government of India in such a way that it inspired a whole new field of bad economics invented by the author of this book, but named by Professor Krueger after studying India. It is called rent-seeking. It also prevented India from using its highly educated population and other assets for rapid growth. The new government, a few of whom were graduates of the London School of Economics and many of whom were devout Hindus, eliminated many of the rent-seeking features of the economy and in fact actually encouraged growth. Today India, instead of being a laggard, is competing with China for the title of the most rapidly growing country in the world.

In both cases there was a period of disastrously bad economic policies. The rent-seeking society of India was more than matched by the famine inspired by Mao Zedong. In many ways a period of disastrous economic policies, although it promotes much suffering, makes it possible to have a rapid growth when good policies are adopted; you are so far behind that rapid growth is easy.

If we look around the world we will see a number of wealthy countries, most of which are democracies. Not all, of course. Tiny Singapore is a dictatorship, and in many ways a model for any country that wants to have an efficient economy. This is, I think, simple luck, however. Their first dictator was a remarkably good economic manager. Apparently the throne is to be hereditary and his son is also a good economic manager. The more normal dictatorship is economically badly managed.

But still, the wealthy countries, with the exception of Singapore, are mainly democracies. They are not in general growing rapidly but that is because they are already well enough off that rapid growth is difficult. China and India can simply copy things that have been developed elsewhere. A wealthy country like the United States or England can in fact grow even wealthier, but rates of growth like those found in China and India are much harder. We have to invent and implement new policies or new technologies if we want to become even wealthier, and that is more difficult than copying.

The subject of this book, however, is not strictly speaking economic growth. It was an effort to introduce the methodology of economics to politics. Most of our present countries that are already democracies could improve their government by a careful reconsideration of the political structure they now have through an introduction of methods drawn from this recent science of public choice. This would mean that they would be better off in many ways, and probably could expect more rapid growth in their living standards as well as greater political freedom. Still, rates of growth like those now found in China and India require not only good economic government, but also for the countries seeking them to be well behind the leaders.

This essay is not intended to indicate that improvements are impossible in the wealthy and free countries. They can both become more wealthy and improve their political structure. An important, even vital, step in that direction is careful study of the new field of public choice and implementing policies drawn from it. I hope that this reprint of what is now a rather elderly book will be a further step in that process.

In the 30 years since this book was originally published the subject of public choice has flourished. Not only is there a sizeable and prestigious journal published in the United States under the name *Public Choice*, but there is also the European-based *Journal of Public Finance and Public Choice*. In addition articles in this tradition are regularly published in other journals, mainly economic journals. The subject has not yet made a large impact in pure political science.

There are active researchers in the field in Japan, Korea and Taiwan, and I fully expect them to develop in mainland China. A former president of the Public Choice Society is a professor in Australia's leading university and hence is able to ensure that the field is active there. This book is a good introduction to public choice as it was 30 years ago, but oddly enough it is also a good introduction to the present field. There has been a good deal of progress and new ideas have been produced, but there have been no radical changes.

We use statistics more and the analysis has been applied to countries that do not speak English, but basically this little book will still give a good introduction to the field. A student who wants to become a genuine expert will have to read many other books, some by me. But this book will not only start him on his way but will give him the basic ideas so that he can not only follow the more recent work but make contributions himself.

Altogether, I think that the decision of the IEA to bring out a new edition is not only sensible but actually a major contribution. Members of public choice societies will probably not want to get involved in serious study but they can recommend it to beginners. Missionary activity in a new field is always helpful for the progress of science. This easy-to-read introduction should be a big help in such activity.

GLOSSARY
(in order of reference in the text)

Public good: A commodity or service which, if purchased for society, must of necessity be available for consumption by everyone. The classical example is the national defence force, which can hardly defend Smith without also defending his neighbour, Jones.

Median voter: The voter in the middle, i.e. the voter who has as many voters on either side of him. In multi-dimensional applications, the median voter has to have the same number of voters on either side of him in all directions.

Pareto optimality: A situation in which it is impossible to benefit one individual without injuring another. Although it seems a very abstract concept, it has turned out to be of great use in formal economic reasoning.

Welfare: A technical term meaning whether or not one has achieved Pareto optimality. The use of the word 'welfare' or 'welfare impact' in this sense may seem misleading to the layman and I do not wish to defend its use, but it is normal in economics.

Bell-shaped curve: Mathematically, a perfectly symmetrical random process generates a curve which looks rather like the cross-section of a church bell; hence the term 'bell-shaped curve' or 'normal bell-shaped curve'.

Two-dimensional analogue: (of the median preference theorem): The median preference theorem was first proved only in a one-government activity space. The two-dimensional variants shown in Figures 3 and 4 (pp. 54 and 56), however, depend on essentially the same proof, albeit in a much more complicated form. The proof still indicates that the voter who is in the middle of the distribution will control the outcome.

Maximand: Something to be maximised; more broadly, a goal or something the individual wants as much of as is possible.

Consumer surplus: The advantage a consumer receives from buying something at less than its maximum value for him: if I would be willing to buy a candy bar at 15 pence but can get it for 10 pence, my consumer surplus is 5 pence.

Production function: Economists' jargon for a complete schedule of the cost of producing various outputs by any enterprise. The words sound clumsy, but there does not seem to be anything else in the English language which means the same thing and which is as concise.

Perfectly discriminating monopolist: A monopolist who can increase his profit by 'discriminating', that is, charging different people different prices for the same product; in the 'perfect' situation, it would mean charging individuals different prices for different units of the product. If I would pay 20 pence for one bar of candy and 15 pence for a second, while Jones would pay 14 pence for one and less than cost for a second, the perfectly discriminating monopolist would charge me 20 pence for my first candy bar, 16 pence for my second, and would charge Jones 14 pence. Needless to say, perfectly discriminating monopolists exist only in theory, but discriminating monopolists as opposed to perfectly discriminating monopolists do exist: the British water industry is an example.

Pork-barrel: American political term for legislation which benefits local areas. Traditionally, rivers and harbours were the basic area for pork-barrel activity; in recent years the term has been used for a much wider scope of activities.

FIGURES

1 ECONOMICS AND POLITICS

The economic view of politics has usually been associated with Marxist thinking. This paper uses a totally different method of analysis. Chapter 1 is a brief introduction to and summary of work done long after Marx, the bulk since 1960, to apply essentially economic tools to the analysis of political behaviour.

Adam Smith, the founder of scientific economics, was a philosopher by profession and interested in many subjects. Although his great contribution was in what we now call economics, he taught in other subjects, including politics. During the 19th century, however, the interest of his followers and economists generally narrowed, and until very recently they largely confined themselves to the study of what is now generally referred to as economics, the analysis of the system of production and distribution. Most economists thus studied the functioning of the market. But there were exceptions: some were interested in the functioning of a centrally-planned economy. Others were concerned with the government as a provider of goods and services, and as a tax collector. Characteristically, their branch of economics was referred to as public finance, and, in practice, until very recently, it concerned itself mainly with problems of taxation.

Most people think the largest single use of traditional economics in the public sector is 'macro-economics' – the economics of unemployment and inflation on a national scale. Although economists were to some extent interested in macro-economics from the very beginning, there was a very large concentration of interest in it from about 1940 to about 1970. In recent years there has also been a lot of application of economics to detailed studies of individual government policies. It seems that economists can provide a good deal of guidance, although seldom final decisions, for such problems as the optimal mix of fighter planes, the number and distribution of hospital beds, etc. This paper is not relevant to any of these traditional concerns of economics. In a way it is antagonistic to them.

The benevolent despot – and the end of illusion

In all such applications of economics, the economist has been concerned with determining an optimal government policy, granted certain objectives, for example, low unemployment, moderate inflation, or defence at the lowest cost. The new economics approach to politics, which was substantially developed in the University of Virginia in Charlottesville, Virginia, is the analysis of the functioning of government itself, i.e. the process by which government makes decisions. In a sense, the traditional economists had what might be called the 'benevolent despot' model of the political order. They have thought their duty was to determine the optimal policy and recommend it to the government, which would adopt it and faithfully carry it out.

Economists in the USA and lately in Europe who are now analysing politics, and indeed the political scientists now rapidly learning economics in order to apply the same tools, have no such illusions. They are characteristically interested in improving the efficiency of the government and have no objections to advising on, say, the internal organisation of the post office; but their primary research is the internal working of government itself, not its output. Government is seen as an apparatus, like the market, by which people attempt to achieve their goals. Instead of assuming that government aims at some particular goal – say, the most health per pound of expenditure – and then calculating how it should be achieved, students of economics of politics assume that all the individuals in government aim at raising their own utility, that is, serve their own interests within certain institutional limits, and then inquire what policies they can be expected to pursue.

Insofar as the new economists suggest improvements, they are normally structural improvements in government. Most of the students in the subject would, for example, favour a much more decentralised government. Although in a small minority, I favour a two-thirds rather than a simple majority in Parliament for most legislation. Forms of government and voting systems were not the kind of problem with which traditional economists dealt. A few years ago they would have been very doubtful whether economic tools could be used to analyse either the functions of government or electoral systems.

Enter the political scientists

Although the new approach to politics originated among economists, before it was very old it also attracted political scientists. Both groups found it was necessary for them to do a good deal of study in the other discipline in order to use economic methods on traditionally political problems. The intellectual retooling was perhaps a little more severe for the political scientists than for the economists, but both had much to learn.

As the former editor of *Public Choice*, the journal of the 'movement', I can testify that about 45 per cent of the members of the Public Choice Society are economists, about 45 per cent political scientists, and the remainder are drawn from other subjects such as philosophy and sociology. Today it is not possible to tell whether the author of an article using economic tools in political science was originally an economist or a political scientist. Indeed, economists from the Virginia Polytechnic Institute or political scientists from the University of Rochester in the State of New York (the two strongest centres of the new work) may study from much the same books, although with a different concentration. Most, however, are scholars who started out in one of the two subjects and have been attracted into the inter-disciplinary work by what they (and I) see as a better explanation of politics than can be obtained from either economics or political science alone.

To date, the work has been theoretical and there has been relatively little empirical testing. This does not reflect an aversion to empirical work. Theories must be invented before they can be tested, and new theories frequently are hard to test. The appropriate data have not yet been collected, and in some cases new statistical methods are necessary. Yet there has been enough empirical testing to confirm the general structure of the new theory.

To give but a few examples, issues of *Public Choice* have included articles on 'A Clear Test of Rational Voting', 'Information and Voting: An Empirical Note', 'An Economic Analysis of Government Ownership and Regulation: Theory and the Evidence from the Electric Power Industry', and 'A Description and Explanation of Citizen Participation in the Canadian Municipality'.[1]

Ethics in political conduct

It is unfortunate but true that the economic approach to politics raises ethical issues. Much of traditional political science was devoted to determining the morally correct policy to be followed in a given inquiry. This kind of issue will not be much discussed here, not because I object to morally correct policies, or even that I do not have views on what policies are morally correct, but because people differ about what is morally correct, and some 2,000 years of debate in the Christian era does not seem to have had much effect on this difference. It does not follow, of course, that the morally correct policies cannot be produced, but it does indicate that, on the whole, we are not likely in the near future to reach general agreement on the morality of egalitarian policies, or the death penalty for

---

1   Jeffrey W. Smith, 'A Clear Test of Rational Voting', *Public Choice*, No. 23, Fall 1975, pp. 55–67; Robert Tollison, Mark Crain and Paul Pautler, 'Information and Voting: An Empirical Note', *Public Choice*, No. 24, Winter 1975, pp. 43–50; Louis De Alessi, 'An Economic Analysis of Government Ownership and Regulation: Theory and Evidence from the Electric Power Industry', *Public Choice*, No. 19, Fall 1974, pp. 1–42; and Mark Sproule-Jones, 'A Description and Explanation of Citizen Participation in a Canadian Municipality', *Public Choice*, No, 17, Spring 1974, pp. 73–83.

murder, or 'just' war versus pacifism, etc. It therefore seems sensible to at least try another approach. Economics has sometimes been claimed to be amoral, although its defenders normally say that giving people what they want seems morally right. The new economic approach to political science can be subjected to the same criticism and defended in the same way.

The economic approach to political problems – like the economic approach to the more traditional economic problems – is not in any sense immoral in itself. Democratic political structures are examined in terms of how well they can be expected to get for the people what they really want. Some social scientists regard this as a low objective, and feel that government should give the people what they *should* want. Normally academics or politicians who hold this view are quite willing to lay down exactly what the people should have. I frequently feel that other people would be better off if, instead of doing as they wished, they followed my advice; but in a democracy there is not much we can do about imposing our view upon the people. They will vote to obtain what they want, not what we think they should want.

Voters and customers: choosing the best bargain

Voters and customers are essentially the same people. Mr Smith buys and votes; he is the same man in the supermarket and in the voting booth. There is no strong reason to believe his behaviour is radically different in the two environments. We assume that in both he will choose the product or candidate he thinks is the best bargain for him.

Although it seems very modest, this indeed is a very radical – even if obvious – assumption. For decades, the bulk of political science has been based on the assumption that government aims at higher goals than individuals aim at in the market. The voter is sometimes assumed to be aiming at achieving 'the public interest', the man in the shop his 'private interest'. Is this true? Is he Jekyll and Hyde?

The private market provides all sorts of opportunities for people who wish to sacrifice their well-being for the benefit of others. There is an immense collection of private charities to which they can contribute money or time.[2] But they do not put a very large part of their income, time, etc., into them. People are interested in the well-being of others, but, except for the immediate members of their families, less intensely than in their own well-being. As a result of empirical research, I once concluded that the average human being is about 95 per cent selfish in the narrow meaning of the term. Of course, many are less selfish (and many are more).

Talking and acting: academics and grocers

There is a sharp contrast between the way people act and the way they talk. It is particularly striking among academics, where discussion of the desirability of making sacrifices for others, striving for abstract moral goals, and in general living a highly virtuous life, is combined with behaviour which is not one whit less selfish than that of the average grocer.

The intellectual history of this fascinating subject is that up to about 250 years ago most discussion of economics was based on the assumption that businessmen were, or at least should be, trying to do their 'social' duty: there was 'the just price' and various moral duties the business community was supposed to perform. One of the great achievements of the late English Enlightenment (in particular of Adam Smith) was the realisation that we in economics did not have to make this assumption. Accepting that most in business are there most of the time to make money, even if they then give part of it to charity, permits more accurate analysis of their behaviour than supposing they are attempting to achieve 'the just price'. Further, in practice the behaviour of the businessman is morally quite respectable, if not saintly. In the course of the pursuit of his private profit, he produces values for other people and, with improved institutions, can be led to produce even more.

---

2 *The Economics of Charity*, Readings No. 12, IEA, 1974, discusses charitable giving in Britain and the USA. My contribution there analysed the functioning in practice of government redistribution in a democracy.

Politicians/civil servants and lesser mortals

On the whole, we would hope the same would be true with politics. There is certainly not much difference between politicians and civil servants on the one hand and the rest of us. A businessman who has been very successful as head of a large firm may change his job to head of a Department of government, but there is no reason to believe his basic character has changed. The conditions under which he operates change, and this should have led to some change in his behaviour, but he was essentially the same man.

In addition to being a US government employee as a university professor at a state institution, I am also on the board of directors of a small company in Iowa.[3] As far as I can see introspectively, there is no difference in my character when sitting with my fellow directors and when carrying out my duties as a university professor. The conditions under which I operate are, of course, somewhat different, and hence my behaviour is not identical; but basically I am the same man.

Both the market and democratic government are institutional structures through which the bulk of us, as customers or as voters, try to achieve our goals. The bulk of us also, as producers, find ourselves employed either in the private or the government sector; and most of us in both are also primarily seeking personal goals. As a general proposition, we shall achieve the well-being of society for the most part only if there is some private benefit for us in taking action to that end. Once again, let me emphasise that almost everyone is to some extent interested in the well-being of others and in various abstract goals, like the 'public interest'. Almost everyone is, in practice, willing to make some (usually rather modest) sacrifices to those ends. This is true, however, just as much of people in private as in government employment.

The difference between government and private employment is simply that the limitations within which the individual operates differ. In general the constraints put upon people's behaviour in the market

---

3   Dodger Products, Eldora, Iowa: we have about 150 employees.

are more 'efficient' than those in government, with the result that individuals in the market are more likely to serve someone else's well-being when they seek to serve their own than they are in government. Indeed, one of the objects of the economic approach to politics is to invent reforms that would raise the 'efficiency' of government closer to that of the private market.

This short paper, written mainly for the newcomer to economics and the general reader, cannot cover the entire work of a large number of scholars who have been working in the subject area of public choice. My outline sketch of the basic argument assumes that if the reader is interested he will turn to the 'Note on Further Reading' for a guide to further material. I shall try to avoid the mathematics which is a prominent feature of public choice. My object is to introduce the subject to people who are not familiar with it. I hope specialists who read the paper will recommend it to their students and to their colleagues in other subjects as an introduction to a still relatively new but rapidly developing branch of economics that is yielding new insights into the working of government.

2   WHY GOVERNMENT?

Among modern social scientists there are devout believers in a centrally-controlled economy who would regard the title of this section as expressing bias. They feel that it is the market, not the government, that must be justified. I should, therefore, say at once that I propose to demonstrate that part of society should be left to the market and part dealt with by government. Since this paper deals with the economics of government rather than the market, it seems sensible to explain why some functions should be controlled by government rather than why some should be controlled by the market; but this is merely a matter of style and not of substance. Readers who wish to assume that government is the norm and the market should be adopted only when there are special reasons for it will find the reasoning fits this approach.[1]

The dawn of 'externalities'

David Hume began the discussion of 'externalities'. As an example he used a meadow[2] which was badly drained and the value of which could be increased by drainage by much more than the cost. If the meadow is owned by one man, there is no problem. He drains it and takes the profit.

---

1   In London in the 1930s there was a debate between professors William Hutt and Abba Lerner on capitalism *versus* socialism. Hutt argued that everything should be done by the market except those activities which are better handled by government. Lerner argued that everything should be done by *government* except those activities better done by the market. The approaches were from the opposite extremes, but both indicated much the same policies in the government/market mix.

2   David Hume, *A Treatise of Human Nature (1740)*, ed. L. A. Selby-Bigge, Clarendon Press, Oxford, 1960, p. 538.

If the meadow happens to lie across the property of two people, they can agree between themselves about the division of the cost and profit of drainage. If many people own pieces of the meadow, agreement becomes extremely difficult. Each person is aware that if he does not contribute to the drainage, his abstention only very slightly reduces the resources available. Further, he will get his share of the benefit at no cost. Individuals are therefore sensible to engage in hard bargaining about their participation in the project and so no agreement may be reached and the meadow may remain undrained.

There are only 20 people or so in Hume's meadow; in government activities there may be millions. Until World War II, London was noted for its pea-soup fogs and pulmonary disease. The cause was soft-coal fires. If everyone switched to other fuels, everyone would benefit; but no individual could benefit *himself* noticeably by stopping, because the reduction in the total amount of coal smoke put into the atmosphere when *he* switched to electric or gas fires was insignificant. A private agreement in which everybody stopped using coal fires would therefore have been impossible.

Hume recommended, in these circumstances, the use of government.[3] Even if the individuals could not agree among themselves on who was to put up what sum of money for draining the meadow and who was to get what parts of the profit, they might have been able to agree to let this decision be made in a more or less automatic way or by an agency thought to be 'impartial'. The agency would not have perfect knowledge about the situation of the individuals, and hence its decisions would be, in a sense, inferior to those from bargaining *if* it worked perfectly.

The decision to adopt a collective method would not be because the outcome is thought superior but because it guarantees an outcome at all. The collectivity can *coerce* the individuals into giving up their private bargaining strategies and accepting an imposed solution, which, although not perfect, could be better than no solution at all. This

---

3   David Hume, *ibid.*

reasoning is particularly obvious in the London coal-fire problem. Clearly nothing could be done by purely private action; the only alternative was a collective solution through government. It should be noted, however, that the government solution was by no means perfectly fitted to the desires of various individuals. Thus, there was inefficiency in the government solution, although much less than if the problem had been left unsolved.

'Externalities' and government

These effects are called 'externalities' in economics. We may have a set of property institutions such that some of the effects of the activity (or inactivity) of a few people are apt to fall on many. The smoking chimney is a classic example. In these circumstances, the people normally cannot come together to bargain on the methods and costs of abatement of the smoke, drainage of the meadow, or the innumerable other objects which governments satisfy. They therefore turn to a collective instrument which performs the function with some (although not impressive) efficiency.

There is nothing in the analysis so far about the 'public interest'. Some governmental activities (such as an adequate police force) are so broadly beneficial that one can reasonably refer to them as being 'in the public interest'. But even here 'the public interest' is simply the sum of the private interests. I would rather not be burgled, mugged, murdered, or subject to embezzlement and fraud, and I presume the same is true of the reader. These desires are just as 'selfish' as my wish for a pay rise.

There is no reason to believe that government reaches perfect solutions either. The number of cases where economists have argued that the market is imperfect and *therefore* recommended that government should deal with the problem is very large. The British economist A. C. Pigou and the American Professor Paul Samuelson both made this error. They *assumed* that government reaches a perfect solution.[4] No one really

4   A. C. Pigou, *The Economics of Welfare*, 4th Edn., Macmillan, London, 1938; Paul A. Samuelson, *Economics: An Introductory Analysis*, 3rd Edn., McGraw-Hill, New York, 1955, pp. 271–72.

believes this, but economists frequently recommend government action simply because the private market creates externalities, and hence is not likely to function perfectly. This is clearly a mistake; we should compare the likely errors of both in the real world and use the institution which will cause less inefficiency, whether government or the market. Where there are large externalities we would anticipate that the private market would not do well. This is called 'market failure' in the technical-economic literature. We must then consider whether the governmental process will do better, or less imperfectly. There is a legend of a Roman emperor who, being asked to judge a contest between two singers, heard only the first and gave the prize to the second, assuming he could not be worse. This is not an optimal selection procedure. We must ask: what are the defects *in practice* of the governmental process compared with the defects of the market?

Defects of government: public goods – all or nothing

The defects (and the advantages) of government provision are discussed later. A few can be dealt with here. The first defect is simply that government, of necessity, buys a single quantity of any 'public good'.[5] When I buy something in the private marketplace, I can decide *how much* of it I want. If I club together with my neighbours to buy a public service, I have to accept the quantity decided upon by the majority (or other) rule in the collective decision process of representative democracy.

I may prefer to pay somewhat higher taxes and have a larger police force with the concomitant lower crime rate; you may prefer a lower tax rate, a smaller police force, and a higher crime rate. If it were possible to buy police efficiently in the private market[6] (I do not believe it is), we could each have our optimal quantity. If it must be bought collectively,

---

5   Glossary.
6   [In *Theft in the Market*, Hobart Paper 60, IEA, 1974, Dr R. L. Carter argues that *some* police services could be bought privately, e.g. cash carrying and other manned security services and detailed advice on crime prevention.]

however, we have to reach a compromise, which may be your optimum, my optimum, or in between; but in any event we will not have our individual optimum, as we would if we bought in the private market.

A second disadvantage is that some people simply dislike uniformity, regardless of quantity or quality. They would not wish to receive the same quantity or quality of services as other people, even if by coincidence it happened to be that which they would choose themselves. This may be a fairly small cost, but it is not negligible.

Since government activity imposes costs in this sense, it does not follow that we should not use the government for some activities. There are also costs in the use of the market process. We must measure and compare the costs in both, and choose the institution which, for the purpose in hand, is the more efficient. To make this decision rationally, we have to consider externalities or other defects in the private market, and the conditions that lead to inefficiency in government provision. We listen to *both* the opera singers and choose the one with the fewer defects. An engineer choosing between a diesel engine and a steam turbine knows that neither of them is perfectly efficient and, for some purposes, one works better than the other. That neither institution is perfect is no argument for not making a choice, but it is an argument for careful calculation of all effects, good and bad. The whole point of the new economic analysis of politics is that it makes these calculations easier, more complete and more accurate.

Changing choice between market and government

There is no reason why the choice between government and market should be permanent or unchanging. Technological changes could increase the externalities where they had previously been low or, perhaps, make it easier for government to produce a good solution. In either event, this would argue for transferring a service previously provided through the market to the government. On the other hand, a sharp fall in the externalities, or a development which made it harder for government to make an optimal decision, would both be arguments for transferring an activity from government to the private market. In a well-functioning polity, activities which had been private 100 years ago would not necessarily be private now, and activities which had been conducted by government 100 years ago would not necessarily still be governmental now, except by coincidence.

As the size and general vigour of human civilisation grows, it has more harmful effects on the environment. A small community surrounded by wilderness can afford to dump all its waste into a stream, while collecting all its drinking water upriver from the dumping point. As the population around the stream increases, this procedure becomes costly. Since government's method of dealing with the problem will not be perfect, it is not sensible to introduce government until the pollution in the stream becomes considerable. Eventually we would reach a stage where the potential costs from inept government action would be less than the current cost from the pollution. Governmental control would then become preferable.

I am an avid reader of science fiction. Suppose someone invents a small, compact, and inexpensive household and industrial waste dispenser which will convert all the waste at very low cost into saleable fertiliser. Since this is a superior system, households and industries begin switching to it from their traditional methods of waste disposal. After a while, the continued existence of the (local) government agency for refuse collection will inflict more costs on society than the little pollution that would be dumped into the stream if the agency were abolished. At that time, the activity should be shifted back to the private market.

My waste disposal device may never be produced, but technological improvement may often call for reduced governmental control. Immediately after World War II, when new television stations were being started in the United States, there was a strong likelihood that they would interfere with one another; their watching areas overlapped on the same wavelength. The regulatory institution chosen to deal with the problem was the Federal Communications Commission (FCC), which had been performing the same function for radio. It did an outstandingly bad job of allocating and policing the TV wavelengths. The result is that Americans have markedly less choice of TV programmes than they could have, and that choice is warped by the FCC's eccentric ideas of TV programming. Yet, while many would prefer better regulation,[7] no one has argued that broadcast TV should not be regulated.

Another way of propagating a TV signal is by cable. There is no reason whatsoever why it should be regulated nationally, but the FCC does regulate it and there is no doubt that its regulation retarded the rate of growth of cable television. The original application of the FCC to TV wavelength allocation was sensible, if not optimal. With the development of new cable technology, the market should have replaced government. Unfortunately, our institutions have not yet been adapted to the changed conditions. And that in itself – the resistance to winding down government even when it has been made out-of-date – is an aspect of the economics of politics.

Once again, this is simply an example. There are many services in which government is less harmful than the market, and many where the market is less harmful than government. We should seek an optimal combination by carefully offsetting the costs in one instrument against those in the other.

---

7   One other regulatory technique would have been simply to sell the wavelengths on the open market.

3 VOTING AS A MEANS OF COLLECTIVE CONTROL

(The diagrams and accompanying text may be skipped by readers who prefer to follow the argument in words. The main conclusions are stated at the end of the chapter.)
We now examine the functioning of government through the eyes of an economist. We deal only with democracy because it is only in democracies that this kind of subject can be studied and because we know more about them than about despotic forms of government. This is not a judgement that democracy is more important than despotic government. Throughout substantially the whole of history the bulk of the world's population has lived under dictatorships of one sort or another. Nevertheless democracy is the system in the UK and the USA, and the only method of obtaining popular control of government that has been tried.[1]

The simplest form of democracy is what we may call the town meeting. It was used by most of the ancient Greek city-states, and it is to this day used by some cantons in Switzerland and by some local governments in the United States.[2] The use of referenda, which are rare in Britain but common in Switzerland and moderately common in the United States, is similar. In most of the democratic countries, the town

---

1   To keep the discussion suitable for a reader without much mathematics, I omit the very difficult problems raised by the so-called 'paradox of voting', which suggests the possibility that no voting rule produces stable results. Since these problems are not only abstract and mathematically difficult but currently the subject of considerable research, leaving them to the specialists seems a sensible approach. It is possible that a new discovery in the economics of politics will invalidate not only this section but, indeed, the whole idea of democratic government! Riker and Ordeshook, cited in the 'Note on Further Reading', discuss the subject.

2   Sometimes in the form of 'town meetings', as in the State of New Hampshire.

Figure 1   **Collective control by voting (police services)**

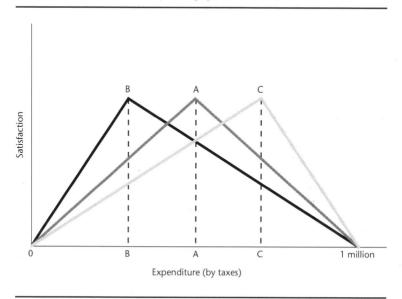

meeting form of 'direct' government has been replaced by 'indirect' representative democracy – a very complicated system.

The median voter theorem

For simplicity, assume a small community in which the basic decisions are taken by direct vote of the citizens. A possible issue is the amount of police services. In Figure 1, the horizontal axis shows various possible expenditures on police services from zero to 1 million. The individual voter, Mr A, will take into account both the costs of possibly being a victim of crime and the tax cost of maintaining the police services. As the police force is expanded, he is less likely to be a victim of crime, but his tax bill will go up. At first, as we move above zero, his total satisfaction increases as we enlarge the police force, because the gain he receives from a reduced crime rate is more than the cost to him of the taxes.

Eventually, however, as the police force grows larger and larger and his tax bill swells proportionately, he reaches the point where he feels that any more police service is not worth its cost. For Mr A in Figure 1, this is at A.

The inverted V with its point at A is a graphic way of representing A's relative satisfaction with various police budgets.[3] Two other voters, Mr B and Mr C, appear on the horizontal axis with an optimum expenditure for each. Suppose our community, Messrs A, B, and C, make decisions by direct voting in open assembly.[4] It is obvious that the median voter,[5] Mr A, will achieve his optimal preference. If A's police budget is placed against any larger police budget, i.e. some point to the right of A, both A and B will be opposed to the change, and only C at the most will favour it. Thus, there will be a majority for point A. The same line of reasoning applies for any lower budget than A.

This simple proposition is the so-called median voter[6] theorem, which simply states that if a number of voters with different views on an issue choose by majority voting, the outcome will be the optimum of the median voter. This theorem is immediately applicable to any odd number of voters; and for large even numbers of voters the slight inaccuracy generated by the possibility of a tie is insignificant.

This result may seem trivial. On the contrary, it has turned out to have surprisingly powerful predictive value. A good deal of empirical research, primarily in the United States, has been built upon this model,

---

3   For mathematical purists it should be emphasised that the vertical dimension of Figure 1 is an ordinal rather than a cardinal dimension. All the lines show is that as Mr A moves from A in either direction, his satisfaction declines continuously. We do not have to say anything about the speed of decline. These lines could be quite irregular, instead of straight, without affecting the reasoning that will follow. The absolute height of the peak also means nothing.

4   I assume here simply majority voting. It is by no means obvious that this system is optimal. Indeed, one of the more interesting aspects of the economics of public choice is the investigation of optimal voting rules or constitutions. The interested reader will find it discussed in J. M. Buchanan and Gordon Tullock, *The Calculus of Consent*, University of Michigan Press, Ann Arbor, Michigan, 1962 (2nd Edn., 1965).

5   Glossary.

6   The median voter is midway in the total range (according to opinion on the policy).

which has been found of great value in predicting[7] the size of school budgets, government policies on conservation, etc.[8]

The median voter model is eminently 'positive' (or what economists used to call behaviourist): it simply predicts what the outcome will be, i.e. how people will behave, without making 'normative' statements about its desirability or undesirability. Some political theorists, sociologists and others tend to feel it is undesirable that the average man gets his way; but in a democracy he frequently does. In considering whether a voting scheme which chooses the median option is desirable or not, we should first notice that, strictly speaking, it does not pass the test of what economists call Pareto optimality.[9] It could be that Mr B feels much more strongly about the issue than either A or C, and hence that some point between B and A would be 'better' than A. This issue is dealt with below.

If the voters have roughly the same intensity of feeling, or if they are randomly distributed, so that people at the left of the midpoint have about as many who feel strongly as people at the right, and assuming that the location of the optima is roughly symmetrical, the median voter preference will be the point of minimum disappointment, i.e. which inflicts the least aggregate dissatisfaction upon society as a whole. The point cannot be proved rigorously without mathematics, but it is intuitively obvious for our three-voter society in Figure 1. As you move left from point A, for example, the satisfaction of B rises but the satisfaction of both A and C falls. On the average, then, this should lead to a fall-off in satisfaction over the group as a whole, although of course with a small number of voters, such as three, none of us would be very happy with taking a statistical approach.

---

7   By building econometric models around this idea.
8   Political parties regularly attempt to stay near the centre of the distribution of voters for this reason. A strong public statement of this position was made by President Gerald Ford, who once remarked: `We are going to stay in the middle'. (*Washington Post*, 10 August, 1975, p. 1.)
9   Glossary.

Figure 2   **Many voters (police services)**

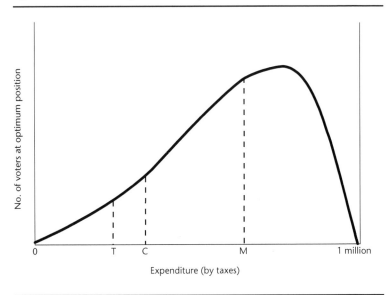

Let us temporarily ignore the 'welfare' impact[10] of this model and attempt to see what we can deduce from it about real-world politics. To make it easier to deal with more realistic problems, we can convert our diagram to another form. In Figure 2, the vertical axis represents the number of voters who have their optimum at any given appropriation level for police services.[11]

Although the reasoning in this section will not be affected by the shape of the distribution of voters, this is because we assume the voter always votes for the alternative from among any two that are put up to

---

10   Glossary.

11   I have drawn this line in as a somewhat skewed normal curve, but nothing much fol-lows from this. For the reasoning to be used in most of the remainder of this section, the reader can draw in any curve he wishes, although it will be necessary to adjust the rest of the diagram to conform. For theoretical research, I usually recommend the use of a flat horizontal line, i.e. the assumption that there are as many people at one point on the issue dimension as at another.

vote which is closest to his optimum. If we assume voters sometimes do not vote at all, or they are confused when two choices are too close together, the distribution of the voters becomes important. These problems require more mathematics. They do not, however, raise any difficulties in principle for the type of model we will use here. I have inserted the median voter at point M on Figure 2; there are as many voters to his left as to his right. The median voter is not at the high point of the distribution and, indeed, would not be unless the distribution happened to be a perfectly normal bell-shaped curve.[12]

Tendency to median 'consensus'

It is relatively rare in modern democracies for government to depend on direct votes of the citizens for the bulk of their decisions. The two-party system with disciplined parties, however, works much the same way. If the parties would rather be elected than beaten, and they choose their policies accordingly, they would attempt to take the position of the median voter, because that assures them of success against any other policy taken by the other party. In practice, of course, we observe that in most two-party democracies the parties are very close together and near the dead centre of opinion.

Once again, this decision of the parties can be criticised, but the party managers, in seeking re-election and choosing their policies accordingly, are creating what advocates of democracy are supposed to favour, i.e. government in which the will of the people counts – heavily.

If there are more than two parties in the legislature or, as in the United States, party discipline is lacking, the median preference model will apply within the legislature itself, with the median individual party (in a multi-party system) or legislator (in the American system) dominating. Congressmen in the United States attempt to follow policies in the legislature which will please the median voter in their constituencies,

---

12   Glossary.

Figure 3   **Joint decision on fire and police services**

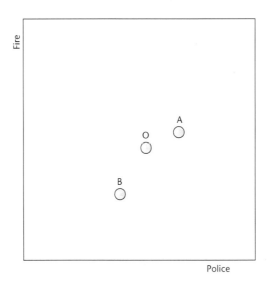

with the result that the median congressman is not too far from the median voter of the country as a whole.

Politicians, like everyone else, make mistakes and on occasion will adopt policies far from the optimum of the median voter. Suppose the leader of one party makes a mistake and comes out for a very small police budget, with its accompanying high crime rate, taking position T in Figure 2. The leader of the other party will not take the median position at M, but will move over in the general direction of the opponent's position, taking up position C. In these circumstances both parties are offering the voters less police protection and a higher crime rate than the median voter wants. Yet this response to the first party's initial error will maximise votes for the second party.

Normally we expect politicians to be reasonably skilful, and hence to adopt positions close to the preferences of the median voter. But this result applies only with two parties. If there are three, and the voting process is like the one used in Britain and the United States, i.e. the candidate with the largest number of votes wins, regardless of how small, 'models' of the sort we have been discussing do not predict any stable outcome. It is possible to compute an optimal strategy for a given party, granted the other two have taken a known stand; but we cannot predict the location of the three parties. By complicating the model a little we can easily accommodate three or more parties. I shall first use a more complicated model, to deal with a two-party rather than a three-party situation.

Two-party system

Figure 3 shows on one axis expenditures on police forces and on the other axis the expenditure on the fire brigade. The individual citizen-taxpayer who benefits from both the police and the fire services, but has to pay for them, has an optimal combination of police expenditures, fire expenditures, and the tax (in Figure 3 it is at 0). At this stage we assume that the individual, in choosing between two budgets which cover both police and fire services, *will* choose that closer to his optimum. For example, he would prefer A to B. In these circumstances, if we place all of the optima on a figure such as Figure 3, then, if we want to find whether A or B would attract a majority of the votes, we can do so very easily by dividing the space into those parts that are closer to A and those parts that are closer to B, and then count the number of optima in each.

If there are many voters, we would not insert the points, but use a method of showing their total distribution, such as contour lines. (I assume the voters are evenly distributed over the space, because it makes the reasoning easier. The same conclusions can be reached with a more realistic distribution of voter optima, but it requires advanced algebra.)

Figure 4 is an example. I have marked the two 'policies', L (say, Labour) and C (say, Conservative). The straight line slanting across the diagram is halfway between the two points and perpendicular to the line between them, and hence divides points closer to L from those closer to C. (If drawn correctly, it exactly bisects the issue space.)

Figure 4   **Fire and police services with two parties**

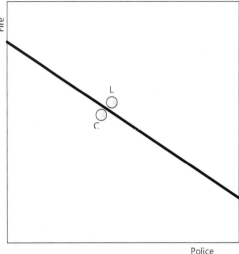

This is a two-dimensional analogue[13] of the median preference theorem described above and can be rigorously proved, as indeed it can be proved for any number of dimensions. We would anticipate that the two parties would be found close together near the centre of the distribution of the voters, and that they would split the voters about 50-50 unless one of them had made a mistake and wandered off from the centre, with the result that the other, by moving in his direction, had succeeded in obtaining more than a majority.

Three-party system: polarising party wings?

The major advantage of using a two-dimensional diagram is that it permits us to discuss more than two parties. Suppose, now, that there are

---

13   Glossary.

Figure 5   **The choice of fire and police services with three parties**

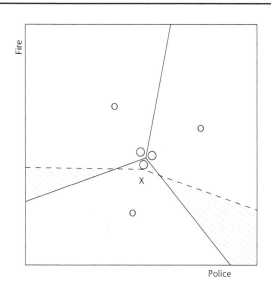

three parties and that we follow the voting system in the United States and Britain under which the party with the most votes wins the election, regardless of whether it has a majority over the other two parties.[14] At first glance, it might appear that the three parties would cluster at the middle in order to attract the most votes, just as two parties tend to be very close together. This is not so. In Figure 5 the location of three parties is shown by the little triangle of dots, and the voters who favour the one closest to their optima are divided among them. What happens if one of the parties moves a little away? Assume that the lower of the three parties moves to the position shown by the X. We can now determine the number of voters who are closer to X than either of the two parties who

---

14   The situation in the United States and Britain is somewhat complicated because this rule applies only in individual constituencies. At our present level of abstraction, this raises no difficulty. The use of the continental type of proportional representation, however, is rather more elegant conceptually and rather more readily analysed.

have not changed their location, and this is shown by the dotted line. The party which moved away from the middle lost votes in the centre of the distribution, but picked up votes around the edge (represented by the shaded areas), and the net result for this move was a gain.

It is not true, of course, that as the parties move out they continue to gain. After a while they move far enough out so that the losses balance the gains from a movement farther out, and the three parties establish equilibrium in locations roughly like the three Os in Figure 5. Thus, one anticipates that the parties in a two-party system would be very close together but that there would be considerable difference between them in a three- (or more) party system. This is what we observe in the real world.

A three- (or more) party system requires a good deal more skill on the part of the party leaders, and mistakes are much easier to make. In a two-party system there is a simple operational rule for the politician: find out what the other party is doing and take a position very close to it in the popular direction. With a three-party system, nothing so simple exists. Difficult decisions must be made and frequent errors are to be expected.

The voter's interest: one main issue

So far I have been assuming that the voters are equally interested in all issues, i.e. as you move away from their optimum point in any direction, they are equally disappointed. In the real world, voters frequently are much more interested in one issue than another: housing, taxation, freedom, overseas aid, etc. In these circumstances, the job of the politician is somewhat more difficult than we have shown here. Anyone who has observed real politicians in action sees how they solve the problem. They try to give to minority groups with strong preferences in one item, say agriculture, favourable treatment in it, and then hope that the group will accept relatively unfavourable treatment in other issues where its feelings are less intense. Analysing this problem in models of the sort developed here is not difficult, but it requires more than two dimensions (which means we should have to proceed from geometry to multidimensional algebra).

The rules deduced for the situation in which all the voters are equally interested in all the issues continue to apply if we consider it from the standpoint of the politician himself. He should select that point in the issue space (Figures 4 and 5) which will attract the largest number of voters: if there are only two parties, we will find him selecting positions very close together; if more than two, the parties will be farther apart.

Power – or the public interest?

This analysis of the politician's tactics indicates simply that he is attempting to be re-elected to office, not that he is attempting to maximise the public interest. We think this situation is realistic, and, in particular, that politicians trying to be re-elected are more likely to be re-elected than those who are not. In the 1960s and 1970s, Goldwater, McGovern and Enoch Powell demonstrated the fate of politicians with strong policy ideals who tried to persuade the voters of their truth. Although all three had considerable national attention, none rose to supreme power. In the same era, Wilson, Nixon, Johnson and Heath were examples of politicians who reached the top, and we doubt that anyone will claim they were highly motivated by devotion to a consistent set of policies. It is true they normally talked in terms of policies, but the policies they favoured changed depending on where political support was to be found. Later, in the 1970s and 1980s, politicians with strong principles were elected in the UK and USA, though it was a short-lived phenomenon.

There is no reason why we should be disturbed by this phenomenon. The market operates by providing a structure in which individuals who simply want to make money end up by producing motor-cars that people want. Similarly, democracy operates so that politicians who simply want to hold public office end up by doing things the people want. Perhaps the people are badly informed in their choice of policies, but all a democracy can really guarantee is popular control, and politicians whose motives and methods we have analysed do give the people control.

4   BUREAUCRACY

Bureaucrats are like other men. This proposition sounds very simple and straightforward, but the consequences are a radical departure from orthodox economic theory.

If bureaucrats are ordinary men, they will make most of (not all) their decisions in terms of what benefits them, not society as a whole. Like other men, they may occasionally sacrifice their own well-being for the wider good, but we should expect this to be exceptional behaviour.

Most of the existing literature on the machinery of government assumes that, when an activity is delegated to a bureaucrat, he will either carry out the rules and regulations or will make decisions in the public interest regardless of whether it benefits him or not. We do not make this assumption about businessmen. We do not make it about consumers in the market. I see no reason why we should make it about bureaucrats.

Bureaucrats and businessmen

A businessman, in an environment that is reasonably competitive and without severe externalities, will normally make a decision which is more or less in accord with the well-being of society, but not because he is consciously *aiming* at the public good. His general aim is simply to make as much money as he can,[1] and he makes the most by doing what

---

1   In practice, and especially in the short run, this general long-run objective may be quali-fied by other purposes: a wish to avoid antagonising colleagues, staff, trade-union organ-isers, suppliers, customers; to gain power or prestige or influence with government; etc. Economists allow for non-monetary objectives. As Alfred Marshall put it, economists suppose only that men try to maximise their *net* (monetary less non-monetary) advan-tages.

is in the social interest. The bureaucrat will also do what is in the social interest if the constraints to which he is subject are such that his own personal interest is identical to the social interest.

The theory of bureaucracy should be based upon the assumption that bureaucrats are as self-seeking as businessmen, and it should concern itself with the design of constraints which will make the bureaucrats' self-interest identical with the interests of society. We should not expect the identity to be perfect – we do not have perfection in the market – but we should expect at least a high correlation. Unfortunately it is harder to arrange such a high correlation in a bureaucratic context than in the market. To return to the main theme of this paper, since we have no perfect solution we must choose among imperfect instrumentalities. What, then, are the imperfections of the bureaucratic process?

Bureaucrats and elected representatives

In most modern countries, an immense number of decisions are taken by bureaucrats. They are supposedly in accord with the decisions of the elected representatives in democracies (or of the dictator in despotisms); but often the influence of these representatives is in practice modest. Indeed there seems now to be developing a mystique under which the bureaucrats are not even supposed to be under the control of elected officials. In an example from the time at which the first edition of this monograph was published, one of the criticisms of President Nixon during the Watergate affair was that he was trying to bring the bureaucrats under his control. The view that many decisions should be separated from political control by being put solely under the control of bureaucrats (sometimes in that oldest branch of the bureaucracy, the judiciary) is still widespread today.

Motives of bureaucrats

What does happen in a bureaucracy? What are the motivations of bureaucrats? Like everyone else, bureaucrats presumably try to improve their own utility. Their utility, again like everyone else's, is partly based upon their immediate ability to consume goods and partly on their appreciation of good things happening to other people. In other words, they are partly selfish and partly public-interested.

In most business activities, the approximation that the businessman is trying to maximise his money income turns out to work rather well, although seldom perfectly. In the bureaucracy, we would like a somewhat similar approximation. If we look over aims in which a bureaucrat might be interested, we can begin by listing those which are of primary concern to him: his salary, his conditions of work, office furniture, etc. (strictly apportioned according to rank in most bureaucracies), his power over other people, his public respect and reputation. In addition to these self-regarding values, let us assume he is also interested in the public good and consciously wants to accomplish something in his job. We can easily think of circumstances in which the two would be in clear conflict. Mr James Smith, for example, is due for promotion to department head, a job which will lead in due course to his becoming Sir James; but Mr Charles Brown is the best man for the job. It is, on the whole, doubtful whether Mr Smith will bring that truth firmly to the attention of his superiors.

On the other hand, we can easily find circumstances where Mr Smith would, for purely *selfish* reasons, be motivated to serve the interest of society. If we assume in this example that he is much abler than Mr Brown, his *selfish* motives would point in the correct direction.

(One of the advantages of the simple profit-maximising assumption in business is that it permits us to assume a single 'maximand'[2] and make calculations. If we consider the businessman as maximising his utility – Marshall's net advantages – we no longer have as easy a problem. His utility is, to him, a simple 'function' which he can maximise; but, to us as outsiders, what is observed is a number of different elements, such

---

2   Glossary.

as his income, respect in his profession, other aspects of his office, etc. We would have to work out a complex function of all those variables and then attempt to maximise it; and this complex function would have to be identical to the one he uses in utility maximising. In general, economists have abandoned this problem, and assume a simple, single goal: the profit. The loss in accuracy is fortunately slight.)

What does the bureaucrat try to maximise?

Is there a similar maximand we can use for bureaucracies? The answer is, unfortunately, 'No', if we want to be completely general. Bureaucrats tend to maximise different collections of activity. But it is true that if we confine ourselves to the type of bureaucracy found in most Western countries, there is a 'not bad' approximation: *size*.

As a general rule, a bureaucrat will find that his possibilities for promotion increase, his power, influence, and public respect improve, and even the physical conditions of his office improve, if the bureaucracy in which he works expands. This proposition is fairly general. Almost any bureaucrat gains at least something if the whole bureaucracy expands. He gains more, however, if his Ministry expands, and more yet if the *sub*-division in which he is employed expands.

I have confined this proposition to *most* bureaucracies in *modern Western democracies.* It is not necessarily true of all these bureaucracies, or of bureaucracies in other political systems. The real issue here is whether the reward structure in the bureaucracy is such that people gain when their burden expands. This is not necessarily true everywhere. Further, there is one important limitation on profit-maximisation which also applies to size-maximisation for bureaucrats: in general, people do not like hard work!

A bureaucrat ordered to do research on, say, improving the bid process for North Sea oil is presumably not totally uninterested in discovering a better method of letting the bids; but he is apt to give more consideration to the opportunity this project gives him to expand the size of his office, and hence improve his probability of promotion, prestige, etc. However, it is by no means certain that he will work hard to achieve either of these goals. Indeed, in the pathological case, he will devote the bulk of this time to essentially leisure activities (some of which, like reading history or solving crosswords, may be located in his office), and time he devotes to work will be solely devoted to an effort to expand his office with no concern at all for its ostensible object. In the more normal non-pathological case, although he may not engage in what we would normally refer to as hard work, he will devote a good deal of attention both to improving the bid process and to using the project to expand his office.

Assume the bureaucrats are simply attempting to maximise the size of their bureaucracies and leave aside, for the time being, their desire to consume leisure (technically described as 'shirking' in the management literature). Economists have gone a long way with their simple, one-argument 'utility function' for businessmen (profit-maximisation); if we cannot get as far with our one-argument utility function for bureaucrats (size-maximisation), at least we should make some progress.

Improving the bureaucracy

One way of improving the size of a bureaucracy is to do a good enough job so that people want more of the activity it is producing. The famous Liverpool Bath would no doubt have continued to function indefinitely, and might even have had a number of additional employees and a promotion for its head, had they been able to make it attractive enough to capture a large number of customers. It does not seem likely that they would have succeeded, but undeniably there are many cases in which individual bureaucrats, whose simple motive is to expand the size of their bureaucracy, are motivated – at least to some extent – to improve efficiency and provide good service.

To examine the matter a little more formally, assume that a government activity, say police protection, is produced at constant cost, represented by the horizontal line on Figure 6. The demand for it (DD) should

Figure 6   **Supply and demand for police services**

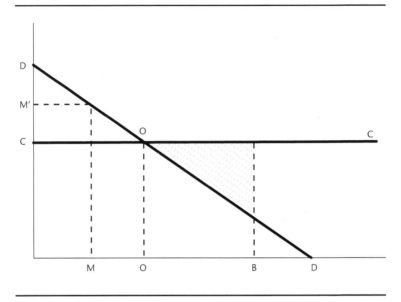

slant downward as in Figure 6, and can be thought of as a demand of the citizenry, or of the higher level of government, i.e. the legislature or, perhaps, of the cabinet.

The usual way of organising and supplying the police is to create a series of regional monopolies, all the police in, say, Liverpool being organised under one control. It has its own decision-making process and its own ends (although much writing on administration implicitly assumes otherwise).[3]

If it were somehow possible to buy police services competitively,

---

3   Two classical sources are Leonard D. White, *Introduction to the Study of Public Administration*, The Macmillan Company, New York, 1948, and William E. Mosther, J. Donald Kingsley, and O. Gleen Stahl, *Public Personnel Administration*, 3rd Edn., Harper and Brothers, New York, 1950. For the same attitude in military administration, J. D. Hittle, *The Military Staff: Its History and Development*, Military Service Publishing Co., Harrisburg, Pa., 1949. This attitude may be found widely spread through the literature; for an example, Mike Royko, *Boss: Richard J. Daley of Chicago*, New American Library, New York, 1971.

individuals buying them and competing companies supplying them, the optimum amount would be obtained at point o, the cost would be the rectangle below and to the left of point o, and the consumer surplus[4] generated for the citizenry shown by the triangle DCO.

If we assume the citizenry continue to buy police services independently (we are assuming this is technologically feasible), but they are supplied by a profit-maximising monopoly, it would provide M units of police service at a price of M', and make a profit equivalent to the rectangle above the cost line and to the left of line M. There would still be some consumer surplus, but clearly the consumers would be in a much worse situation than with competitive suppliers.

Let us now more realistically assume that the individuals are not purchasing the police services as individuals but through a governmental agency which has a demand for police services derived from the demand of the individual citizens. The supplier is also a monopoly: there is only one police force in Liverpool; and let us assume that the police attempt to maximise the size of their bureaucracy. What is the likely outcome?

Single buyer v. single seller

First, we have a monopsony (single buyer) against monopoly (single seller), and this is always a difficult situation for economists to analyse. What would happen if one or the other of the two had everything his own way? If the legislature is in complete control of the situation and has a perfect idea of the cost structure facing the police, they could offer the rectangle left of and below o to the police in return for the police producing o amount of police protection, and we would have the same solution as in free competition.

If the police have everything on their side, which means they are able to conceal their own cost from the legislature, they can misrepresent the cost of providing various amounts of police services, and the

---

4   Glossary.

legislature will not be able to discover their true 'production function'.[5] We then get a most extraordinary situation. The police will provide B police services and charge the amount of the rectangle under the cost line and to the left of B. This means that for the marginal police services they are charging more than they receive and there is a net social waste shown by the shaded triangle. They are able to get away with this, however, because the size of the shaded triangle is the same as DCO. As a perfectly discriminating monopolist[6] always will, they have squeezed out the entire consumer surplus, but have spent it on providing additional police services.

How do we reach this conclusion? The police department is not assumed to be profit-maximising (it is not possible for the policemen simply to pocket any profit they make), but they are benefited in various ways by the expansion in the size of the force. Since we assume that they are exploiting the demand curve to the maximum, they are also maximising their size by this socially wasteful expansion.

This situation is the ultimate result which could be expected if the bureaucracy worked hard at expanding its budget and was able to exploit the full monopoly gains in all-or-nothing bargaining from the legislature. The taxpayer would be indifferent between the existing police force and no police force at all, which, of course, also makes possible much lower taxes. It seems doubtful whether any existing bureaucracy has reached this position. Many bureaucracies, from the standpoint of the citizen-taxpayers as a whole, may be beyond this point; but that is because they are satisfying the demands of some persistent and voluble minority. In these circumstances, a true demand curve would be that of the minority and, once again, I doubt whether many real-world bureaucracies have succeeded in exploiting their monopoly positions to the full.

There are a number of reasons why bureaucracies would not be able to reach this goal with any degree of regularity. First, and obviously, the

5   Glossary.
6   Glossary.

legislature or purchaser of the services from the bureaucracy characteristically has at least some information about the production function of the bureaucracy and is not subject to what we might call 'complete' exploitation. Secondly, since the members of the bureaucracy among other things want leisure, they are unlikely to put in the concentration and hard work required to exploit the legislature to the theoretical maximum.

Ironically, the desire for leisure – what we normally call laziness – has a net benefit for society. Suppose the individuals in the bureaucracy work hard enough to get only 80 per cent of what they could if they devoted full force to achieving it. The cost level line in the diagram would be adjusted upward to indicate that you have to hire more policemen to get a given amount of protection. This clearly would be a disadvantage for the taxpayer-citizen. On the other hand, the bureaucracy in negotiating with the legislature would not get all of the welfare triangle; it would leave 20 per cent of it to the citizen. The citizen would therefore derive some benefit from the service, although if the policemen were energetic and hard-working in both 'policing' and exploiting the legislature, the consumer surplus would be entirely consumed in producing 'efficiently' police services not worth their cost. The citizen taxpayer is better off with lazy servants than with diligent ones here, but this results simply because the diligent ones will use their diligence to extract surplus value from him.

Odds with the bureaucracy

Does the bureaucracy in practice extort its entire theoretically possible gain from the legislature? This is the classic monopoly-against-monopsony problem, and economists normally say it is insoluble. But there are good reasons for believing the odds will be heavily on the side of the bureaucracy. It will have a good idea of the legislative demand for its services, which is essentially derived from the voters' demand. The bureaucracy has access to the newspapers, television, etc., and therefore has a good idea of the popular demand. In the circumstances, the legislature is not able to keep its demand curve a secret.

These factors are exaggerated by two special characteristics of governmental demand. First, most government demands are organised by special interest pressure groups, like the farmers, who normally are intimately connected with the bureaucracy which will carry out the policy, which, in turn, is therefore very well informed about the political pressures that can be brought to bear upon Parliament and the government. Secondly, a good part of the demand for bureaucratic services comes not from the people who will *receive* them but from those who will be paid to *supply* them. The bureaucrat who works for the ministry dealing with policy in agriculture, or the policeman who works for the chief constable, is also a voter. In voting, he (and his family) have two demands for their bureaucracy's service. First, they, like other citizens, gain whatever benefits it generates; but, secondly, they gain privately from the payments made to them.[7]

They are part of the demand for their own services, and a particularly important part. They combine very good information about their bureau with strong motivation. And, indeed, they seem to represent a larger percentage of the voting population than of the total population, because they are more likely to vote. Rough estimates in the United States indicate that about one out of five Americans derives his support from a government job in the family, but about one out of four voters does so.

If the bureaucracy has a good idea of the demand for the service, the government has difficulty determining the cost of providing it. In

---

7   This, of course, assumes that the payment to them is higher than their opportunity cost, not a very radical assumption in most modern governments. At the time the first edition of this paper was under preparation, the city of New York, as a result of a fiscal crisis, was talking of firing 10,000 policemen. The police officers' union prepared and circulated to tourists a pamphlet entitled 'Scare City', warning against the dangers of visiting New York City if the police were reduced – an effort to manipulate the demand for their services. Similar episodes have happened frequently in the UK under the Thatcher, Major and Blair governments when cuts in particular public services have been proposed.

general, the only source of such information is the bureaucracy, which is apt not only to say that economies are impossible but also, if economies are imposed, to act so as to maximise their cost instead of attempting to do the best job it can in the new circumstances.

Bureaucrats resist 'cuts' by superior knowledge

Three examples readily come to mind. The first occurred when I was serving on the council of the American Political Science Association (APSA). We were in one of the budget crises which afflict learned societies from time to time. The APSA maintains in Washington, DC, a large office, engaged in not too well defined activities. It was suggested that one of the ways we could escape from our budget problem was to reduce expenses in this office. The permanent secretary of the society, who had been responsible for building up the office after he was appointed, immediately said that 'Yes, that could be done'; it would be possible for him to lay off two or three of the employees in the subscription service branch, i.e. those who took care of seeing to it that everyone got their *American Political Review, P.S.*, and other documents circulated to members. The result clearly would be that members were inconvenienced. He did not suggest that any of the 'policy officials' might be dispensed with, although it was never clear what the bulk of them were doing.

My second example involves the Federal Customs Service. Its budget was reduced. The civil servant in charge laid off every Customs Inspector in the USA but not one person in any other part of the Customs Service. This was too extreme, and he was transferred in a burst of unfavourable publicity; but he was not fired.

The third case concerned newspaper reports that the Immigration Service is deliberately investing its resources in office staff rather than in Inspectors to make it necessary for Congress to increase its budget.

This kind of behaviour is common with bureaucracies; and, in general, congressmen have found it difficult to prevent. Professor William

Niskanen, whose book *Bureaucracy and Representative Government*[8] rigorously develops the size-maximising principle, spent most of his life before writing it as an economist in the Department of Defense, attempting to improve its efficiency. Immediately after writing the book, he moved to a higher-level agency, the Office of Management and Budget, the general control agency of the US government, and found that there, too, it was impossible for him to outmanoeuvre the bureaucrats because they simply knew more about their departments than he did.

Solutions: more information? – reducing bureau monopoly?

What can be done? First, an attempt to develop expertise at the upper layer is required to which the whole development of cost-benefit analysis is directed. More information would help, but it is not obviously going to lead to much improvement. What is needed is some way of lowering the bargaining potential of the monopoly bureaus.

In the market place we do not try to discover the cost structure of companies from whom we buy products or service. All we do is compare the prices and services offered by organisations and choose the one that suits us best. The existence of a monopoly, of course, makes it hard for us to do this, and we tend to feel disadvantaged. Is there some way in which we could provide for Parliament or Congress the same ability to select the lowest price rather than putting upon it the burden of determining the operating efficiency of the bureaucracy? The answer, fortunately, is that such possibilities often exist, and as far as we can tell they improve efficiency.

First, although most government services are produced under monopoly conditions, some are produced with varying degrees of competition. It is very hard to get measures of efficiency, but something

---

8   Aldine-Atherton, New York, 1971; the argument is summarised in *Bureaucracy: Servant or Master?*, Hobart Paperback No. 5, IEA, 1973.

can be done. Examining the data,[9] we find that the least efficient bureaus are those which have perfect monopolies.

Second, where, although the individual bureau has a monopoly in one area, several bureaus operate in different areas, the legislature can at least compare cost curves. The police forces, which in both the USA and Britain are organised as a series of local monopolies (except for privately-supplied police services) rather than as a national service, are an example. There are, of course, many others, such as refuse-collection, fire-fighting, education, etc.

Third, still more efficient are government bureaus which provide a service that is also supplied by private companies. Waste removal in the USA, for example, is sometimes a government activity and sometimes carried out by private companies charging a contract fee. So far as we can tell, the government bureaus, although not as efficient as the private companies (as measured by price and service), are nevertheless markedly more efficient than government bureaus which do not face private competition.

Government bureaus, even in this final negative situation, are almost *never as* efficient as private companies in a competitive industry.[10]

The question of the efficiency of private industry in monopolistic situations, of course, is not at issue here, since no one (so far as I know) regards this as a particularly desirable organisation of the economy. The reason is simple (Figure 6). If one company protected by a high tariff has a monopoly in motor-car production in its home market, the demand curve is for motor-cars in total. If there are two companies, the motorist who is thinking whether or not to buy a car also has the alternative of buying it from the other company. Similarly with a bureaucracy: the more the competition, the more it is forced to produce close to the optimum output and productive efficiency one would anticipate in a competitive industry.

9   Thomas E. Borchording (ed.), *Budgets and Bureaucrats: The Origins of Government Growth*, Duke University Press, Durham, NC, 1976.
10 *Ibid.*

Introducing competition into the bureaucracy
(a) Competition within bureaus

Can we introduce competition into bureaucracy? First, we could simply stop enacting cartel legislation. Most 'efficiency' studies of government[11] have attempted to root out competition (called 'duplication'). In the US automobile market, not only is General Motors 'duplicated' by Ford, Chrysler and American Motors, but a lot of odd foreigners like Fiat, Volkswagen, and Toyota are also 'duplicating activity'. Wouldn't we be much more efficient if we abolished 'duplication'?

The absurdity of this proposition would not in any way be reduced if we substituted a government service for production of motor-cars. In the USA, highways are characteristically constructed by a large number of private companies. Their repair and maintenance, however, is normally done by monopolistic government enterprises. In some areas – Blacksburg, Virginia, where I live, is an example – a good deal of the maintenance is let out on bids to competing private companies. We pay lower repair prices than we would if a monopolistic agency was doing all the repairing. Furthermore, the competing companies ready and willing to replace bureaucracies in other cities and counties also make the road repair bureaucracies there careful about prices.

Thus one way of increasing the competitiveness of government services is simply to contract them out. Many services are contracted out in various places in the world. The entire line of public utilities – telephone, telegraph, radio and television transmission, water supply, sewage removal, electricity, and gas – are sometimes provided privately and sometimes publicly. Usually the private companies are given some kind of a government monopoly, which sharply reduces their efficiency;

---

11 This tradition has been maintained consistently. A very thorough example is the multi-volumed Hoover Report prepared by former President Herbert Hoover for former President Harry S. Truman immediately after World War II, and the almost equally voluminous Ash Report prepared for former President Richard M. Nixon by Roy Ash, formerly the president of a large corporation and, after completing the report, Chief of the Office of Management and Budget. Both reports may be obtained from the US Government Printing Office, Washington, DC.

but sometimes one or more of the utilities are generated by competing private companies. It is not obvious that this arrangement is ideal, but it would certainly be worth careful investigation. The mere act of looking into this possibility would probably lead to very sharp improvements in efficiency in the corresponding government agencies.

There are also many other government activities which can be performed by private agencies on contract. Fire protection is, in general, a government activity, but a private fire protection industry has developed in the state of Arizona. The private fire protection companies enter into contracts with the smaller cities to provide them with fire protection, and also offer their services to private individuals. Comparative studies[12] seem to indicate that the private companies provide fire protection for about half the cost of public fire departments serving similar communities. Further, the private companies – tiny though they are – have been the cutting edge of scientific progress in the fire protection industry. They have invented an entirely new technology which, granted the extraordinarily small funds they have for research, is a remarkable achievement. This technology is beginning to spread through the US government fire departments, but only very slowly, since there are few fire commissioners who really want to cut their budgets in half.

(b) Competition between bureaus

A second way to impose competition on bureaucracies is to retain bureaucratic control but permit competition within it. The area served by a bureaucracy might simply be divided into smaller areas with separate budgets. It would help efficiency if Parliament made a habit of changing the geographic scope of the small bureaucracies handling, say, police protection. If, for example, the Commander in charge of division

---

12 A popular account of this phenomenon is William C. Wooldridge, *Uncle Sam, the Monopoly Man*, Arlington House, New Rochelle, NY, 1970, pp. 124–27. For a more scholarly account, Roger Ahlbrandt, 'Efficiency in the Provision of Fire Services', *Public Choice*, XVI, Fall 1973, pp. 1–15.

I seems to have done better one year than the Commander in charge of neighbouring division II, 15 per cent of II might be added to I, the Commander of I promoted, and the Commander of II reduced. In the following year, at the very least a good deal of thought on methods of improving efficiency by both might be expected. Perhaps the 15 per cent could be shifted back at the end of the next year.

Small-scale experiments desirable

So far we have gone from analysis to a set of reforms which may seem radical. It is generally not desirable to adopt radical proposals instantly for a large and important organisation. Experimentation on a small scale would seem to be called for. The proponents in Britain and the USA of the voucher method of financing school education are a good example. Although they are convinced it is the best method, they are not proposing that the education system be revolutionised, but that well-conceived experiments be undertaken to obtain more information and to find whether their proposals are as attractive in practice as they appear to be in theory. The reforms for bureaucracy should be handled in a similar manner. They can be tried in a local area and, if they work, expanded. As may not have escaped the reader, I think they would work.

5 LOGROLLING

The word 'logrolling' is a fairly usual one in the American version of English and seems unknown in the English version. Its meaning is very simple: I agree to vote for something you want in return for your agreeing to vote for something I want. It is also a very common phenomenon in a democratic political system; indeed, it usually dominates the process of selecting policy although it is concealed from public view.

Logrolling is frequently thought to be wicked and, indeed, is against the law in many democracies. The laws against logrolling (probably passed in part through logrolling) have substantially no effect on the functioning of democracy in countries which have adopted them. At best, they make it necessary to carry on the logrolling in a somewhat indirect and hidden way, which probably reduces its efficiency to some extent. Nevertheless, most people when first told about logrolling feel it is undesirable, yet they normally do not respond in this way if it is explained with a little tact.

A British example

I once attended a meeting where there were several British MPs. One, of outstanding personal ability and with an academic background, seemed a good man to ask about the institutions in Britain. When I put the matter to him, he denied flatly that there was any logrolling; and, after my efforts to explain my hypothesis on how it was done, he denied this was so. Shortly thereafter, he made a public speech in which he explained how he was working to get his party to support a certain policy. The description was 100 per cent logrolling; as he put it, 'I attend committee meetings and vote on things I don't care about at all in order to get the people who really are interested in those subjects to attend my meeting. And then I hold up their hands when it comes to a vote'. The latter, of course, was an exaggeration.

This MP had simply been trained in one theoretical description of how politics works and then learned how politics works in practice. Since there was no reason for him to put these two ideas together, he had not done so. When I, a visiting specialist in the economics of politics, asked questions about British procedure, he answered quite truthfully in accordance with the theory he had learned. When he was explaining what he himself did, he again truthfully explained, but was not aware of the divergence. It was not until after his public meeting, when I raised the issue, that he realised there was any contradiction between the two positions.

Logrolling in Labour and Conservative politics

My friend the MP was typical. Most people who deny the existence of logrolling in what we may call the theoretical context either engage in it or expect that their representatives will engage in it in practice. The 'social contract' in Britain, for example, if one accepts the Labour Party and trade union description of it,[1] involved an exchange of redistributional policies for union support. Union support is supposed to take the form of not making too large wage demands, but it is nevertheless a policy swap. But I have seen no public claims that it is immoral. It is sometimes said it will not work, or that it is fraudulent in the sense that neither party really intends that it shall work. This is quite different from saying that the social contract would be immoral even if it were completely successful.

Conservative Party politics at the same time raised something like the same issue. After being elected party leader, Mrs Thatcher promptly intro-

---

1   This was a policy followed in Britain in the mid 1970s.

duced into her Shadow Cabinet a number of people who had opposed her when running for the leadership. She also quickly moderated her political position so that she would acquire more votes, and hence have a better chance of applying her policy. The various factions of the Conservative Party who backed Mrs Thatcher then clearly found themselves, when the Conservatives formed a government, required to vote in Parliament for some policies they did not like in return for receiving others they did like but to which other groups in the party objected.

All of this is perfectly normal, not only for British politics but for democratic politics in general. Indeed it is also normal for non-democratic politics, although we know less about them, and hence it is not so clear there. In all democracies I know of there is both public criticism of logrolling as immoral, as well as the widespread use of it in making government decisions.

Explicit or implicit logrolling: a US 'model'

Logrolling is usually classified as either explicit or implicit. Explicit logrolling is more common in the USA than in Britain, but it is a little easier to explain if we begin with an explicit 'model' and then proceed to an implicit 'model'. So, although this paper is to be published in Britain, let me begin with the American Congress rather than the British Parliament, and simplify matters by assuming there is only one legislative house.

If we examine the day-to-day process of government in a democracy (or, indeed, a non-democratic government), we observe that most of the activities have differential impact: they affect some people more than others. A proposal to change the tax law will have more effect on some citizens than on others. Almost all expenditure decisions affect some citizens more than others. Even simple changes in the criminal law are usually of differential effect.

These observations are not necessarily obvious to the casual observer. 'The public works budget', 'the military appropriation', 'the health programme' appear to have wide scope if we think of the whole programme at once. In practice, detailed decisions must be made, such as where to run a dual carriage highway (which makes a lot of difference to many people because of the effect on the value of their homes), which weapons system the armed forces will purchase, and where new hospitals will be built.

These policies can be dealt with by establishing general rules. But the details become important to special groups and, in any event, democracies do not seem to be able to stick to general rules. Referring them to non-political officials may be a solution, provided they are convinced the elected officials will not take their performance into account when deciding on such matters as departmental appropriations.

Differential impact of political decisions

We cannot avoid such differential impact of decisions (although we can avoid *thinking* about it). But it is not obviously undesirable. Suppose all government acts were decided by direct majority vote, with all individuals voting on them. Some of the smaller Swiss cantons come very close to this system. Suppose there is a project which would benefit one city, say Durham, very much and which would have a relatively modest cost to the national taxpayers. If Durham were unique, i.e. if there were no other city which could receive a major benefit at modest cost to the national taxpayers, we might feel that the nation should not make this gift to them. But in the real world, such situations are common. There are many opportunities for investment in public facilities in local areas for which the cost is less than the benefit. If they are to be paid for from the national exchequer, however, and if they are voted on individually, they would most assuredly fail.

Suppose the benefit to Durham would be £100 million and the tax cost is £1 per head for all UK voters. If we put it up to a direct vote, the voters in Durham, facing a very favourable 'trade-off' of a £1 expenditure against a large return, would presumably vote for it. The taxpayers in the rest of the UK, facing a cost of £1 which does not benefit them at all, would surely vote against it. And the project would be lost. We deal with these problems by setting up a kind of bargain, explicit or implicit, in which Durham gets its project and a lot of other cities get theirs.

In the US Congress, this bargain is fairly open and above board. The bulk of the negotiations take place in committees, cloakrooms, and congressional offices, but there is no secret about what is going on. In the traditional 'pork-barrel'[2] area of public works, suppose we are 50 years in the past and President Eisenhower has decided that dual carriage highways be built in various parts of the USA to improve highway transportation. They are to be paid for (as indeed they were) by a tax on the gasoline consumed by *all* drivers – not only those who drive on the dual carriage highways.

In these circumstances, a given community is best off if it has one of the interstate roads running through it, but it must also pay for interstate roads built in other parts of the country. One would anticipate that the congressional delegation from, say, Pennsylvania would, on the whole, favour interstate highways in Pennsylvania and, to some extent, those outside; but, generally speaking, they would not be interested in taxing the inhabitants of Pennsylvania to build 'interstates' 3,000 miles away in California. In the event, Eisenhower met this problem by implicit logrolling, rather than explicit. But it is a nice example to explain explicit logrolling also; so let us discuss it as if it had been decided by explicit logrolling, and then switch to explain implicit logrolling.[3]

Explicit (open) logrolling

If the congressional delegation from Pennsylvania is interested in getting

---

2   Glossary.
3   A study of the way in which the highway system has adjusted itself to the political reality is Ann F. Friedlander, *The Interstate Highway System: A Study in Public Investment*, North Holland Publishing Co., Amsterdam, 1965.

its interstate highway through, it goes to the delegation from Illinois and offers to vote for 'interstates' in Illinois if they will vote for 'interstates' in Pennsylvania. It makes the same kind of trade (exchange, swap) with Texas, New York, etc., until it gets a majority of the Congressmen willing to vote for 'interstates' in Pennsylvania. We now have the 'interstates' being built in Pennsylvania and a number of other states have the Pennsylvania delegation's promise to vote for their highways. The delegation from, say, Illinois already have the Pennsylvania vote and require others. They seek out, say, California, Oregon, Florida, etc., until they also compile a majority.

There is no reason in this type of (explicit) logrolling why the coalition that votes for the Illinois roads should be the same as for Pennsylvania. Indeed, we would anticipate that almost all the states would be able to build up this kind of coalition simply because a state that seemed to be on the verge of being left out could offer exceptionally good terms. It could, for example, take somewhat fewer miles of road in its own state, and hence impose a lower tax on citizens in other states, or it could 'sweeten' the bargain by promising to vote for something else of special interest to another state in addition to their roads. The end-product should be an 'interstate' network spreading all over the USA in a way which fairly uniformly reflected the number of voters in each state.

Although this was not the way the interstate was laid out in the USA, the *nationalestrassen* in Switzerland are being built almost entirely in this way: by explicit logrolling. This is why *nationalestrassen* are highly disconnected. It is necessary to give at least a few miles of divided highway to mountain cantons, such as Chur, if their support is to be obtained for the *nationalestrassen* running through heavy-density areas such as the plateau between Lake Geneva and Lake Konstanz.

Implicit ('secret') logrolling

In the USA the interstate system was built by a special form of implicit logrolling. A professor at Harvard, who had been deeply involved in negotiating the interstate bill when on leave as a government official, read a book[4] which discusses logrolling on return to Harvard. He informed a number of his colleagues that he had concluded that explicit logrolling was inherently immoral, but that implicit logrolling of the sort used to build the 'interstates' was quite different and moral. He was willing to concede that the end-result was about the same, but thought the means were more important.

Many people, when they finally are willing to concede the existence of logrolling, seem to take the view that explicit logrolling is somehow morally much inferior to implicit logrolling. I have never been able to understand this view, but perhaps the reader will find it congenial. At any rate, this is how implicit logrolling works.

Instead of voting on each segment of the system, it would be possible to vote on the system as a whole. In essence, a network of highways, together with their supporting taxes, was proposed in Congress consisting of many segments. However, the individual voter and taxpayer, instead of having to make up an explicit bargain with other people in which he voted for highways in other states in return for getting them in his own state, could look at the whole collection and decide whether he favoured it or not.

This procedure does not eliminate the logrolling but simply makes it less public. It makes the logrolling implicit. The details of the nationwide highway system and the tax to be used to pay for it must be so designed as to produce a majority of votes. Since it is still true that the citizens of Pennsylvania gain from highways there and, to a lesser extent, from highways in the vicinity, but lose on highways on the other side of the continent, the person who makes up this highway bill, which is a package of individual proposals for construction of highways, must analyse the preferences and the relative intensity of preferences of the citizens of the various states.

The Harvard professor had spent several years in this arduous

---

4   J. M. Buchanan and Gordon Tullock, *The Calculus of Consent*, University of Michigan Press, Ann Arbor, 1962 (2nd Edn. 1965).

activity, and finally he and his colleagues had produced a highway construction bill which could get through. He had gone through a negotiation process very similar to that which would have occurred had we used the explicit logrolling process; but the implicit logrolling was quieter, and more centralised.

It is possibly, though not certainly, more efficient to do it this way because it centralises negotiations in a small group of specialised people.

In any event, the outcome is apt to be similar, except that with implicit logrolling it is possible for a group, which could be almost 50 per cent of the population, to be left out of the bargain. In a way, implicit logrolling moves us back to the median voter situation in a special form.

Logrolling and the median voter

What is the relationship between logrolling and the median voter analysis? The answer is simple if put in geometric terms.[5] In plain English, the difference is that there are some issues upon which people feel much more strongly than on others. It is these issues which lead to logrolling. Individuals are not motivated to make trades (exchanges) between two issues if they all feel equally strongly about both because there is no profit to be made by a bargain. It is only when the two parties feel more intensely about certain issues, and the issues are different, that a bargain can be made. If A is very much interested in having Liverpool harbour dredged at the government's expense and would, on the whole, prefer not to be taxed to pay his share of the dredging of Southampton harbour, he may nevertheless be able to make a bargain with residents of Southampton with the opposite preferences, under which both harbours are dredged. This kind of bargain cannot be presented by simple geometry because it requires more than two dimensions and algebraic tools.

---

5   The indifference curves around the optima in the median voter theorem were circles. In logrolling they are ovals.

Implicit logrolling in Britain: party manifestos and coalitions

The most obvious single case of implicit logrolling is the position taken by a party going into a general election. The manifestos of the major parties in Britain (or the platforms in the USA) show that they involve implicit logrolling. Measures clearly unpopular with many voters are included because they are highly popular with a minority, which can be expected to accept other planks in the platform unpopular with it. In the 1970s opinion polls indicated that trade unions in Britain were disfavoured by a majority. Nevertheless, the Labour Party supported them and the Conservative Party refrained from urging very radical acts against them.[6] The reason is obvious. The strong partisans of the trade unions were likely to vote for the Labour Party because of its support, even if some of the other parts of its policy were contrary to their desires. And other members of the Labour coalition, although they were more critical of unions, were willing to accept a general programme which included support for the unions because other parts of the manifesto promised policies they favoured.

In a sense, almost every bill that passes through a legislative body represents this kind of implicit logrolling. The people who have drawn up the bill have consulted many other members of the legislature and have made changes to please minorities who can be brought to support the bill if given something in return. No doubt the supporters of the bill have also engaged in explicit logrolling in that they have promised to vote in favour of other issues in return for that support.

Referenda

In a way, the clearest example of implicit logrolling will be found in some referenda on local improvements in the USA. Sometimes these referenda involve a large project. The voters in my county in Virginia recently voted against a proposal for a new courthouse. Often the referendum proposal

---

6   Though a series of pragmatic measures did undermine their strength over a long period.

is a collection of unrelated projects except that if grouped together it is thought a majority will favour them, whereas it would oppose any individual one. Since this kind of referendum is frequently used in school financing, textbooks used to teach administrators of public education in US schools of education frequently contain instructions on how to make up this kind of bargain.[7]

We should not be unhappy about these very common democratic practices, although normal discussion of them is condemnatory. There is no reason why minorities should not be served by democracies. The problem is acute only if the advantage to the minority is less than the gain to the majority.

Logrolling in Britain: compromises in the cabinet

The description I am about to give is to a considerable extent hypothetical rather than based on direct personal knowledge. In the first place, I am a foreigner. Secondly, British politics is carried on in a highly secretive manner. It is not very obvious exactly who determines the policies that the parties adopt. It is clear that the party in power will, because of the party discipline that normally dominates the British parliament, be able to get its will enacted. The question is: how does it determine what it 'wills'? There are two possible and different procedures, but fortunately they lead to much the same conclusion.

For the first, let us assume that the basic decisions are made by the government itself, or in practice the cabinet, which is composed of a group of people who (a) are leaders of the party, i.e. represent various points of view within it, and (b) are the heads of branches of the executive government. In both of these capacities, they have ideas on what policy should be carried through. It is only possible, however, for, say, the Secretary of State for Education to get something she favours if

---

7   This is, in my opinion, not to be criticised morally. But another aspect of these textbooks should be severely criticised: they also explain how to time the election so that people who favour the collection of expenditures are more likely to vote than people who do not.

she can win the support of the bulk of the cabinet. As a consequence, an implicit, extremely tactful process of negotiation goes on in the cabinet, and a series of policies are adopted, mainly in the form of bills to be presented for passage by Parliament. If the incumbent wishes to remain Prime Minister and the members of the cabinet wish to remain members of the cabinet, this combination of bills must be such that at least a majority of the party will back it and the members of the cabinet are very good representatives of the politically active part of the party. Thus, a compromise set of bills worked out in the cabinet is apt to be one *which the* party as a whole will regard as acceptable. One Minister accepts a Bill *which benefits* another, but which he would prefer not to pass, in return for the contrary favour to him.

The second procedure by which the same outcome is likely comes through the party apparatus. For example, assume there is a set of committees of MPs who determine policy and who must maintain the support both of their local party apparatus and of the voters. These committees on various subjects do not in the true sense control the cabinet or the shadow cabinet (if the Party is in opposition), but their expression of opinion has strong influence: the members of the cabinet or shadow cabinet hold their positions in essence because they have the support of at least one-half and preferably much more of their MPs.

The procedure is as described earlier. Individual members of the committees have personal preferences. They make bargains with one another (no doubt in a most tactful way) under which they swap support. In consequence, the 'position' (policy) papers adopted by these committees have general voting support, even though the proposition, if taken by itself, would often attract only a small minority of the party.

All of this is strongly reminiscent of the American system, except that it is concealed rather better. The American system is also rather concealed, and frequently congressmen will deny what they are doing. Indeed, a number of political scientists have succeeded in writing books about Congress without noticing the phenomenon of logrolling. This probably reflects their essentially moralistic approach more than their inability to see what is going on before their eyes.

Benefits of logrolling

But if logrolling can clearly create benefits, it can also cause harm. Consider a simple society of nine voters who confront a large collection of measures, each of which will be paid for by a tax of £1 on each of the nine, and each of which will confer benefits exclusively upon one of them. Policy A will cost a total of £9 in the form of a £1 tax on each voter, but will confer upon voter A a benefit worth £15. Clearly we would, on the whole, prefer that projects like this go through, although for any individual bill of this sort we might object to its effects on the distribution of income. Normally we would anticipate that the voters, if confronted only with this bill, would vote eight to one against it; but with logrolling, assuming there were similar projects for other voters, it would get through while conferring similar benefits on other voters. The end-product would clearly be an improvement in the state of society.

But consider another project which similarly imposes a cost of £1 on each of the nine citizens and confers upon voter A a benefit of only £2. Here there is a clear cost of £7 to society as a whole. We would not want this bill to pass. And it would not get through under logrolling because the voter could not afford to vote for four other bills each of which would cost him £1 apiece, in return for four other people voting for his bill. This would lead to a loss for him of a net of £3, and hence he would not attempt to logroll the measure.

Defects of logrolling

So far logrolling has worked efficiently; unfortunately, there is an intermediate class of issues where it does not. Suppose the return to voter A of a bill (which, once again, costs £1 apiece to every one of the nine taxpayers) is £7. He would be willing to trade a favourable vote on four

Figure 7   **The costs of democratic decision**

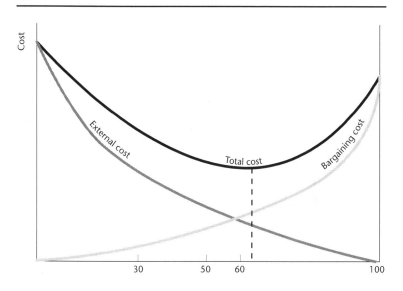

other issues, costing him a total of £4, for four votes on his issue which would net him £2 on the entire deal. Society as a whole, however, would have been paying £9 for something worth only £7. We clearly do not want the government to undertake this kind of action. Is there something we can do to ensure that only those bills with benefit to society get through by logrolling? Unfortunately, the answer is 'No', but we can do better than the present system. I regret to say that the necessary change, however, is one the average person will consider extremely radical.

Before indicating my radical prescription, let us begin with a theoretical analysis. Assume we have very many voters. Let us also consider various possible voting rules other than majority rule. On Figure 7 I have drawn the horizontal line as the possible voting rules that might be adopted: from requiring only one voter at the left to requiring unanimity or all of the voters at the right.

When I first present this diagram to students, I almost always encounter the view that a rule of less than majority is impossible. In the modern world, in which it is very common for candidates or even governments to be elected by less than the majority, as now in Britain, I find it hard to understand this position. Yet it is true that, although less than majority institutions are commonly used for electing *candidates* to office, they are rarely used for selecting *policies* or passing laws.

All recent governments of Britain have had much less than a majority of votes; indeed, none since 1945 has had a majority.[8]

In both countries, the voters vote for someone other than the ultimate government – MPs in Britain, electors in the USA. Yet these representatives are very often elected by less than a majority.

We can use for policies the same procedure we use for selecting candidates. It is true that we will have to abandon the Speaker's casting vote, invented to make a simple majority voting process work. It fits in nicely with majority rule and does not fit in with any other voting method. If we are going to consider other voting methods, we must assume that we use the same procedure used in selecting MPs in England, which is that anyone who wishes to be an MP puts his name up (and a deposit) and the one with the most votes is elected. For issues, anyone could present any proposal for voting and, in a series of periodic rounds of votes, the one with the most votes would be passed.[9]

Another complication is necessary for my diagram, though not for real-world voting. Many real-life voting systems have a minimum number of votes necessary for election. The Peruvian military government of the 1970s, for example, originated in a complicated dispute about whether a person elected to the Peruvian presidency did or did not have the 40 per cent of the popular vote the constitution required. The horizontal line on Figure 7, then, represents all such rules: from that which says the minimum number of votes necessary for an issue to pass

---

8   The American figures are not quite as extreme, but also not drastically different. Since 1870, only two-thirds of all American presidents have had a majority of the popular vote.

9   As is true with the election of MPs, some arrangement to prevent instantaneous reversal by the next vote would have to be included.

is one to the rule which requires 100 per cent. The points indicate the percentage of votes necessary for passage: 50 is, of course, approximately the point normally used in majority rule.

On the extreme left end, the one-person rule would mean that any proposition favoured by any individual in society would be enacted. The £1 tax on all the nine members of our little society required to confer a benefit of £2 on one of them would be accepted under this rule. The 'external cost' line indicates the cost of this procedure. The individual facing any voting system except unanimity will find that some bills are passed which, on balance, injure him. This clearly inflicts a cost on him and is an 'externality' in the same way as the injury inflicted upon him by a smoking chimney.

As the number of votes required to pass a bill rises, the individual must select only those policies for which the cost to him of acquiring support is less than the benefit. The 30 per cent rule, for example, would eliminate our £2 benefit at the cost of the £9 bill, but not the £7 benefit bill. As the number of votes required to pass is increased, the likelihood of the individual being caught by a bill which injures him goes down; hence the external cost curve falls. At unanimity, it is at zero, although there are other reasons for not using unanimity.

If we deal with the kind of bill that does not concentrate its benefit on a few people but spreads it over a number, increasing the number of votes required for passage does not affect it until the number exceeds the number with net benefits. Then they must begin logrolling and, if the total benefit to society exceeds the total cost, they should be able to pass it even if the rule is unanimity. In other words, the external cost line is a genuine statement of the cost inflicted upon people by the passage of bills which, on balance, injure them under the different types of voting rules.

What about bills not passed? Surely they are as important as the ones that are. If we assume that bargaining and logrolling are absolutely costless and instantaneous, no bills for which the total gain exceeds the total loss would ever fail. This assumption, of course, has nothing to do with the real world; it is frequently very useful for analytical purposes and we have used it for the last few paragraphs. Let us now abandon it.

Radical solution: a proposal for 'reinforced majorities'

Another line is marked 'bargaining cost' on Figure 7. If we are following the 'any-person' rule, there is no bargaining cost. I simply specify what I want done and it is done. When we require more voters, however, I have to make bargains with them. In the first place, there are resources committed to the bargaining process. More important, however, as the number of voters increases and in particular as it approaches unanimity, we will find that desirable legislation will fail because the bargaining process is too tedious and expensive. Hence, the bargaining cost line is partially the investment of time and energy in bargaining; but, much more importantly, imposing this bargaining cost means that desirable bills fail.

The total cost inflicted upon society by various rules is calculated by simply summing these two cost lines, as in the total cost line. The low point on this line is the optimal voting rule for the society. Only by coincidence would it be the simple majority. For important matters, I think in general it would be well above the majority and, indeed, most formal constitutions require more than a majority for at least some matters. The British constitution in this respect is something of an exception, but even in Britain so-called constitutional changes are not attempted unless there is thought to be more than a simple majority of support for them, regardless of the technical possibility. Even if republicans some day found themselves with 51 per cent of the MPs, it is extremely doubtful whether they would regard themselves as authorised to dethrone the Queen and confiscate her property.

Majority voting is thus generally not optimal. For important matters we would require something more. This conclusion is in general accord with constitutional processes throughout the world. But my opinion is that 'reinforced majorities', say two-thirds majority, should be used much more widely than they now are. Indeed, I have on occasion recommended that the President of the United States always veto all bills in order to compel a two-thirds vote for everything in both houses of Congress. Startling though this proposal is, the analysis which leads to it is fairly orthodox political economy.[10]

10 [Professor Tullock is, with Professor J. M. Buchanan, the originator of this analysis — ED.]

6 ENVOI

When I began this paper, it seemed to me that instead of surveying the contributions of the new economic approach to politics, it would be better to present a few simple, but fundamental, examples. The reader can get an idea of the type of reasoning applied and some of the conclusions drawn from it. Even at this early stage, the conclusions are by no means uncontroversial; but I think they withstand scientific criticism. I hope I have aroused the reader's curiosity and that he or she will continue studies in this development of economics to government and politics. New knowledge is more valuable if used than if it moulders in a library. (To assist in further investigations, I have appended suggestions for further reading, and in this edition there are also the commentaries by other public choice specialists.)

Today, in both Britain and the USA, there is a widespread feeling that the old solutions have failed. This is a time when a careful rethinking of our position is necessary. I hope the new economic approach to politics will provide the foundations for such a reconsideration.

A NOTE ON FURTHER READING

For the British reader interested in learning more about the new economic approach to politics, a brief introduction to the literature may be helpful. On the theory that the reader of introductory papers does not want to jump immediately into the most difficult and advanced work, I begin with more general books rather than highly specialised texts and journal articles.

On the subject of Chapter 2, there are two general books, *The Logic of Collective Action* (Harvard University Press, 1965) by Professor Mancur Olson, and my book, *Private Wants, Public Means* (Basic Books, New York, 1970). Olson's was the pioneering work; my book, an undergraduate text, may be better as an introduction, even though it contains little original thought. On Chapter 3, Professor Duncan Black's *The Theory of Committees and Elections* (Cambridge University Press, 1958) is the pioneering work. Professor Anthony Downs's *Economic Theory of Democracy* (Harper & Row, New York, 1957) and Professor James M. Buchanan's *Demand and Supply of Public Goods* (Rand McNally, 1968) are also essential.

A discussion of the voting paradox and an introduction to a large collection of other problems raised by voting is in *An Introduction to Positive Political Theory* (Prentice Hall, Revised edn., 1973) by Professors William H. Riker and Peter C. Ordeshook. This is a difficult book, but I know of nothing simpler. *The Calculus of Consent* (Michigan University Press, Arm Arbor, 1962) by James M. Buchanan and me discusses the design of optimal voting rules and other problems of producing a constitution. Although easier than Riker & Ordeshook, it is more difficult than most of the other books I suggest below. Finally, on Chapter 4, my book,

The Politics of Bureaucracy (Public Affairs Press, Washington DC, 1965), and William A. Niskanen's *Bureaucracy and Representative Government* (Aldine-Atherton, New York, 1971), will set the reader well on his way. The reader may then wish to turn to the more specialised literature. Dennis C. Mueller's comprehensive review article and bibliography of public choice is in the *Journal of Economic Literature*. It contains a comprehensive bibliography and surveys a good deal of work I thought too advanced for this paper. As another fairly readily available source, the journal *Public Choice* carries articles published in this subject. Looking through issues will provide an update of the most recent work in the economic approach to politics.

FURTHER READING

Barry, Brian M., *Sociologists, Economists and Democracy*, Collier-Macmillan, London, 1970.

Buchanan, J. M., and Tullock, Gordon, *The Calculus of Consent*, University of Michigan Press, Ann Arbor, Michigan, 1962 (Second Edition, 1965).

Dahl, Robert A., and Lindblom, Charles E., *Politics, Economics and Welfare*, Harper & Row, New York, 1953.

Downs, Anthony, *The Economic Theory of Democracy*, Harper & Row, New York, 1965.

– *Inside Bureaucracy*, Little, Brown & Co., Boston, 1967.

Niskanen, William A., *Bureaucracy and Representative Government*, Aldine-Atherton, New York, 1971.

– *Bureaucracy: Servant or Master?*, Hobart Paperback No. 5, Institute of Economic Affairs, London, 1973.

Olson, M., Jnr., *The Logic of Collective Action*, Harvard University Press, Cambridge, Mass., 1965.

Schumpeter, J. A., *Capitalism, Socialism and Democracy*, Harper & Row, New York, 1950.

QUESTIONS FOR DISCUSSION

1. One of the arguments against electoral reform has been that, in a more representative system, coalition governments would become the rule and voters would not have a clear choice of policies. Do inter-party coalitions pose more difficult problems of choice to voters than intra-party coalitions? Would policies carried out by a coalition government be different from those under the present system?

2. From the point of view of the information available to a voter, which is preferable:

(a) a multi-party system in which a coalition will always be necessary to form a government; or

(b) a two-party system in which coalitions are made within the parties?

Would your answer be different if in a multi-party system every party announced in advance, as part of its platform, the party or parties with which it would be willing to join in a coalition?

3. Anthony Downs (*Economic Theory of Democracy*, p. 297: cf. Further Reading) says: 'New parties arise when either (a) a change in suffrage laws sharply alters the distribution of citizens along the political scale, (b) there is a sudden change in the electorate's social outlook because of some upheaval such as war, revolution, inflation or depression ...' Can you apply this analysis to the rise of the Labour and the Scottish Nationalist parties?

4. What would you predict about the attitudes of the Conservative, Labour and Liberal Democrat parties to Scottish Nationalism assuming that their objectives are to maximise their political power? Specify the assumptions you make about the reaction of Scottish voters to 'nationalistic' policies. How would you expect the existence of a fourth party, the Scottish Nationalists, to affect the attitudes of the other three parties?

5. In the USA many of the higher (and lower) ranks of the 'civil service' are political appointees. When there is a change in the political party in power there is a massive change in the government bureaucracy. In Britain Ministers change but the civil service remains unchanged. Compare these two arrangements, making explicit your assumptions about the goals pursued by the various groups.

6. One of the arguments against private health services has been that they would draw the 'better' resources (doctors, equipment, etc.) away from the National Health Service. One of the arguments against private provision of mail and other government-provided services has been that they would draw away the more 'lucrative' trade. Discuss a similar argument in the following cases: Cinemas draw customers away from TV (and *vice versa*); which should be prohibited? Private house building draws resources away from council house building (and *vice versa*); which should be prohibited? The provision of leather shoes draws resources away from leather furniture; which should be prohibited?

7. When the government considers cuts in public expenditures there are always reports of Ministers fighting for their Departments to be exempted; some even threaten to resign if cuts are made. Is this an efficient way of allocating resources?

8. Discuss the following two arguments:

(*a*) Nationalised industries will be more efficient than private industry because their shareholders (i.e. taxpayers) via their representatives (the government) can fire managers more easily than can shareholders in large private companies.

(*b*) The trouble with nationalised industries is that politicians, for political motives, interfere in their management and do not allow the managers to run them in a 'businesslike manner'.

9. In recent years firms on the verge of bankruptcy (or beyond) have sometimes been saved by the government. What are the economic or political justifications for this? If the justification is political, do you think the different parties would tend to rescue different kinds of firms? What criteria would, and should, be used?

Part 2
COMMENTARIES

1 THE LIFE AND SCHOLARSHIP OF GORDON TULLOCK: A PERSONAL APPRECIATION

Charles K. Rowley, George Mason University

A short biography

Gordon Tullock was born in Rockford, Illinois, on 16 February 1922. His father, George, was a hardy Midwesterner of Scottish ancestry; his mother, Helen, was of equally hardy Pennsylvania Dutch stock. He obtained his basic education in the public schools of that city, displaying from early childhood a superior intellectual ability that clearly distinguished him from his peers. In 1940, Tullock left for the School of Law at the University of Chicago to combine a two-year programme of undergraduate courses with a four-year formal law programme. In fact, he completed the initial two-year programme in a single year.

His law school programme was interrupted by his being drafted into military service as an infantry rifleman in 1943, but not before he had all but completed a one-semester course in economics taught by Henry Simons. This course was to be Tullock's only formal exposure to economics, a fact that no doubt enhanced rather than hindered his future success in contributing highly original ideas in that discipline.

Tullock served in the US military until shortly after the end of hostilities, returning to civilian life in December 1945. He took part in the Normandy landings on D-Day+7 as a member of the Ninth Infantry. His life was almost certainly spared by the good fortune of his being left behind at division headquarters to defend three anti-tank guns. The original members of the Ninth Infantry were decimated on their hard-fought route across France and into Germany.

Following behind, Tullock would eventually cross the Rhine, he claims, while still asleep. Ultimately, he would end up in the Russian sector. Although Tullock modestly dismisses his wartime service as uneventful, this can only be with the advantage of hindsight. Participation in a major land war as part of 'the poor bloody infantry' is never without the gravest of risks.

Following this three-year wartime interruption, Tullock returned to Chicago and obtained a Juris Doctor degree from the Chicago Law School in 1947. He failed to remit the $5 payment required by the university and thus never received a baccalaureate degree.

His initial career, as an attorney with a small but prestigious downtown Chicago law firm, was controversial and, perhaps, mercifully brief. During his five-month tenure, Tullock handled two cases. The first case he won when he was expected to lose, and only after one of the partners in his firm had advised his client not to pursue the matter. The second case he lost when he should have won, and he was admonished by the court for his poor performance (Brady and Tollison, 1991: 2). Fortunately for the world of ideas, these events persuaded him to seek out an alternative career.

Prior to graduation, Tullock had passed the Foreign Service Examination. He joined the Foreign Service in the autumn of 1947 and received an assignment as vice-consul in Tientsin, China. This two-year assignment coincided with the communist takeover in 1948. Following Tullock's return to the United States, the Department of State dispatched him to Yale University (1949–51) and then to Cornell University (1951–52) for advanced study of the Chinese language. In late 1952, he joined the 'Mainland China' section of the Consulate General in Hong Kong. Some nine months later he was reassigned to the political section of the US embassy in Korea. Tullock returned to the United States in January 1955, where he was assigned to the State Department's Office of Intelligence and Research in Washington. He resigned from the Foreign Service in the autumn of 1956.

Over the next two years, Tullock held several positions, including most notably that of research director of the Princeton Panel, a small subsidiary of the Gallup organisation in Princeton. Essentially, he was in transition, marking time until he was ready to make a bid for entry into academia.

Unusually, Tullock had already published in leading economics journals articles on hyperinflation and monetary cycles in China and on the Korean monetary and fiscal system even during his diplomatic service, thus whetting his own appetite for an academic career and signalling an unusual facility for observing his environment as the basis for creative thinking. Furthermore, he had read and had been intellectually excited by the writings of such scholars as Joseph Schumpeter (1942), Duncan Black (1948), Anthony Downs (1957) and Karl Popper (1959), scholarship that provided the basis for reintegrating economics with political science within a strictly rational choice framework. In short, Tullock was ready to play a significant role in extending the empire of economics into the territory of contiguous disciplines.

In the autumn of 1958, at the age of 36, encouraged by Warren Nutter, he accepted a one-year post-doctoral fellowship at the Thomas Jefferson Center for Political Economy at the University of Virginia. Still a relatively unknown quantity at that time, Tullock nevertheless brought with him to the Center two indispensable assets, namely a brilliant and enquiring, if still-unfocused, intellect and an unbounded enthusiasm for his adopted discipline of political economy. Quickly he forged a bond with the director of the Center, James M. Buchanan, a bond that would result in some of the most original and important political-economic scholarship of the mid-twentieth century.

His fellowship year at the Center was productive, resulting in an important publication on the problem of majority voting (Tullock, 1959). In the autumn of 1959, Tullock was appointed assistant professor in the Department of International Studies at the University of South Carolina. Publications continued to flow (Tullock, 1961a, 1961b) while, also in 1959, Tullock crafted a seminal draft paper entitled 'A generalized economic theory of constitutions' that would become the fulcrum for *The Calculus of Consent* (Buchanan and Tullock, 1962).

On this basis, Tullock quickly advanced to the rank of associate professor before returning to the University of Virginia, and renewing his relationship with James Buchanan, in February 1962, just as the University of Michigan Press was publishing their seminal book, *The Calculus of Consent*. In 1966, Tullock edited and published the first issue of *Papers on Non-Market Decision-Making*, the precursor to the journal *Public Choice*. Between 1962 and 1967, Tullock published innovative books on bureaucracy (Tullock, 1965), on method (Tullock, 1966) and on public choice (Tullock, 1967), as well as a rising volume of scholarly papers that earned him international recognition as a major scholar.

Despite this distinguished résumé, Tullock would be denied promotion to full Professor of Economics on three consecutive occasions by a politically hostile and fundamentally unscholarly university administration. In the autumn of 1967, Buchanan protested against these negative decisions by resigning to take up a position at the University of California at Los Angeles. Tullock also resigned to become Professor of Economics and Political Science at Rice University. With Ronald Coase having resigned for similar reasons in 1964 to take up a position at the University of Chicago, it appeared that the nascent Virginia School of Political Economy might have been deliberately nipped in the bud by the left-leaning administration of the University of Virginia.

As a result of a successful initiative by Charles J. Goetz, the University of Virginia plot failed. Goetz succeeded in attracting Tullock to Virginia Polytechnic Institute (VPI) and State University (SU) in Blacksburg as Professor of Economics and Public Choice in the autumn of 1968. Goetz and Tullock immediately established the Center for Studies in Public Choice in 1968, as the basis for promoting scholarship in the field and as a means of attracting James Buchanan to join them at VPI. This initiative bore fruit in 1969, when Buchanan joined the VPI faculty and assumed the General Directorship of the Center, which was immediately renamed the Center for Study of Public Choice. Simultaneously, Tullock renamed his journal *Public Choice* and the new sub-discipline set down fruitful roots in the foothills of the Appalachian Mountains.

Henceforth, Tullock would never again look back. Over the next one third of a century he forged for himself a reputation as a brilliant entrepreneurial scholar and a formidable debater. To this day he refuses to rest on well-earned laurels as a founding father of three sub-disciplines of economics, namely public choice, law and economics, and bioeconomics.

Universities have recognised his contributions by appointing him to a sequence of Distinguished Chairs (VPI & SU 1972–83, George Mason University 1983–87 and 1999–, and the University of Arizona 1987–99). Professional associations have honoured him by electing him to their presidencies (the Public Choice Society, the Southern Economic Association, the Western Economic Association, the International Bio-Economics Society, the Atlantic Economic Society and the Association for Free Enterprise Education). In 1992, an Honorary Doctorate of Laws was conferred on him by the University of Chicago, in 1996 he was elected to the *American Political Science Review* Hall of Fame and in 1998 he was recognised as a Distinguished Fellow of the American Economic Association. These awards and honours reflect powerful entrepreneurial contributions across three major scholarly disciplines.

Tullock as a natural economist

James Buchanan describes Gordon Tullock as 'a natural economist', where nature is defined as 'having intrinsic talents that emerge independently of professional training, education and experience' (Buchanan, 1987). In Buchanan's judgement, there are very few such natural economists, and most of those who claim competence in economics are not themselves 'natural'. Buchanan identifies Gary Becker and Armen Alchian, along with Gordon Tullock, as prominent members of the rare natural economist species.

A 'natural economist', therefore, according to Buchanan, is someone who, more or less unconsciously, thinks like an economist:

> An economist, in the sense of the term used here, views human

beings as self-interested, utility-maximizing agents, basically independent one from another, and for whom social interchange is initiated and exists simply as a preferred alternative to isolated action. (Buchanan, 1987: 9)

As Buchanan recognises, all reputable economists rely on the rational choice model when analysing market interactions. Yet many of them waver or object when extending the rational choice model to the analysis of non-market behaviour. The behaviour of such agents as politicians, voters, bureaucrats, judges, preachers, research scholars, family members, criminals, revolutionaries, terrorists and media anchors, they argue, cannot be captured effectively in terms of the rational self-interest model. The natural economist has no such inhibitions.

As the reader of *The Vote Motive* (1976) will note, Tullock never hesitates to apply *Homo economicus* as the core assumption in all areas of economic analysis. His focus, however, is always on expected utility maximisation rather than narrow wealth maximisation, and, unlike many of his public choice peers, Tullock fully recognises the (limited) relevance of altruism in the individual's utility function (Rowley, 1987).

George Stigler once remarked, in distinguishing his own scholarship from that of Milton Friedman, that whereas Friedman sought to change the world, he (Stigler) sought merely to understand it. This distinction holds equally with respect to the scholarship of Gordon Tullock (Rowley, 2003). Precisely because Tullock seeks to understand – even when what he learns is unappetising – he adopts no subterfuge in his analytical approach.

If consent exists, Tullocks notes and explores its rationale. If conflict is manifest, Tullock investigates the social dilemma to the extent possible with the tools of neoclassical economics. Few judgements are passed; few policy recommendations are advanced. Tullock simply chronicles observed events as part of the diverse universe that he is eager to explore.

Tullock's world view

In many respects, Tullock manifests the characteristics outlined by Buchanan (1987) as defining the natural economist. Tullock is, however, much more than this. He is a warm-hearted and deeply concerned person with a powerful vision of the nature of the good society and a willingness to explore, from the perspective of rational choice, the reforms necessary to move mankind on to a better path.

In this regard, Tullock's philosophy is utilitarian in the modified sense of the Pareto principle, adjusted to allow for individual decision-making behind a veil of uncertainty (Rowley, 2003: 115). This philosophy, first spelled out in *The Calculus of Consent* (Buchanan and Tullock, 1962), has been deployed systematically by Tullock throughout his later scholarship.

Tullock is not an anarchist. He believes that there is a role for the minimal state in protecting the lives, liberties and properties of individual citizens. No doubt the role of the state extends in his mind beyond that of the minimal or 'nightwatchman' state. Any such extension is, however, extremely limited.

Unlike many self-professed classical liberals, Tullock has not allowed himself to be diverted on to a normative Hobbesian path by the events of 11 September 2001. Rather, he has maintained a principled Lockeian position that a free society should never overreact to perceived violence and that basic constitutional rights should not be trampled on. He is a true friend of liberty, always watchful and vigilant in its defence (Rowley, 2003).

Tullock's powers of observation

Among all the economists I know, Gordon Tullock is blessed with the most acute ability to observe his environment meaningfully and to translate those observations into robust research programmes. Such powers are rarely found within the scientific community and, when effectively cultivated, result in major contributions to knowledge.

With respect to this ability to convert acute observation into successful writing, Gordon Tullock closely mirrors the great naval historian, novelist and social satirist C. Northcote Parkinson, whose own writings on bureaucracy helped to trigger Tullock's initial interest in public choice.

Students of Tullock's scholarship quickly recognise that Tullock's first-hand experience of the behaviour of United States diplomats in early post-war China and South Korea manifested itself in his seminal work on the politics of bureaucracy; that his observations of begging in China, of taxicab medallion values in New York City, of restaurant prices in Washington, DC, and of road repair policies in Blacksburg, Virginia, led to important breakthroughs in the theory of rent-seeking; that his observation of contributions to the offertory trays in churches and chapels led to 'Tullock's Law of Wealth Redistribution'; that his observation of the feeding habits of the coal tit led to his seminal contribution to bio-economics; that his observation of the behaviour of ant and bee colonies led to his seminal work on the economics of non-human species; and that his observation of currency expansion and inflation in China and Korea led to his important contribution to monetary economics during the 1950s.[1]

Tullock's successful economic imperialism

In 1992, the Royal Swedish Academy of Sciences awarded the Bank of Sweden Prize in Economic Sciences in Memory of Alfred Nobel to Gary S. Becker 'for having extended the domain of microeconomic analysis to a wide range of human behavior and interaction, including nonmarket behavior'. In the view of the Swedish Academy, Becker's contribution consisted 'primarily in having extended the domain of economic theory

---

1   On these points, see my introductions to the various volumes of *The Selected Works of Gordon Tullock*, including *Bureaucracy*, vol. 6; *The Rent-Seeking Society*, vol. 5; *The Economics and Politics of Wealth Redistribution*, vol. 7; *Virginia Political Economy*, vol. 1; *Economics without Frontiers*, vol. 10.

to aspects of human behavior which had previously been dealt with – if at all – by other social science disciplines such as sociology, demography and criminology'. In so doing, he had stimulated economists to tackle new problems.

Central to Becker's use of the economic approach is his contention that 'the economic approach is uniquely powerful because it can integrate a wide range of human behavior' (Becker, 1976). To this end, Becker's research programme is founded on the idea that the behaviour of individuals and groups adheres to the same set of fundamental principles in a wide range of different circumstances.

Specifically, Becker deploys maximising behaviour explicitly and extensively across all areas of human behaviour, be it the utility or wealth function of the household (and its separate components), firm, labour union, special interest group or government bureau. He assumes the existence of equilibrating markets (usually viewed as being efficient) that both coordinate and constrain the desires of different participants so that their behaviour becomes mutually consistent. The preferences of individuals are assumed to be homogeneous across individuals and not to change substantially over time (Stigler and Becker, 1977). Becker also assumes that all individuals and groups are well informed about the market (or non-market) environment in which they participate (Rowley, 1999).

The assumptions that underpin Becker's economic approach reflect the more general approach of the Chicago School in offering a tight prior equilibrium theory of human behaviour in which markets clear quickly and efficiently and in which changes in outcomes are driven, not by changes in tastes, but by changes in constraints (Reder, 1982; Tollison, 1989, 2003). In this manner, Becker has successfully invaded other disciplines in the social sciences and has used the rational choice approach to advance understanding of human behaviour.

Over the past 40 years, Gordon Tullock has matched Gary Becker in the successful imperialistic invasion of rational choice economics into contiguous social science territories as well as, even more ambitiously, into the natural sciences. As *The Selected Works* clearly demonstrate, Tullock has deployed the rational choice approach of economics to disturb conventional thinking not only in economics, but also in the disciplines of political science, social studies, the law, biology and scientific method. In so doing, Tullock has stimulated other scientists to follow in his path and to shift the direction of their research programmes to explore rich hypotheses that his entrepreneurial scholarship has identified.

The economic approach of Tullock, however, differs in significant respects from that of Becker and, as a result, provides different insights into the predictable implications of human (and non-human) interaction. Tullock retains the *Homo economicus* assumption of maximising and self-seeking man, while being much more willing than Becker to recognise the importance of non-wealth arguments in the individual's utility function.

Tullock also allows for the possibility that political markets will not always clear, and when they do clear that they may do so inefficiently. He allows for the possibility that information will not be widely dispersed in political markets. He allows for differences in individual preferences and for changes in those preferences over time, not least in response to persuasive advertising.

In combination, these assumptions define a diffuse rather than a tight prior equilibrium as the hallmark of Tullock's scholarship (Rowley, 1993, 1996; Rowley and Vachris, 1995, 2003). Political markets are not always in equilibrium, though they do adjust dynamically towards equilibrium. Political market outcomes may be inefficient in allocating resources, and they may offer high-cost solutions. Institutions matter and cannot be ignored. Ideas are important and shape outcomes. In all these respects, Tullock's analysis diverges sharply from that of the Chicago School.

Conclusion

The Vote Motive distils much of the finest scholarship of the early Tullock.

As a monograph it has served magnificently in introducing many students of economics and politics to the basic elements of public choice. Of course, over the succeeding years Tullock has continued to provide significant new insights into non-market decision-making. Without his contributions, public choice most certainly would be a less rich and a less interesting field of scholarly endeavour.

Tullock requires no written testament to his half-century of contributions to Virginia political economy. His testament is in his life and in his work. It is in the enthusiasm of the large number of scholars and students who seek out his company both at professional meetings and in the Center for Study of Public Choice. It is in the heartfelt gratitude of his many friends and acquaintances who dine well at his always generous table (Rowley, 1987).

It is fitting, therefore, to close this assessment of Gordon Tullock and his scholarship with the epitaph engraved on the tomb of Sir Christopher Wren in St Paul's Cathedral: *si monumentum requiris, circumspice* (if you seek his monument, look around). Fortunately for Virginia political economy, this is no epitaph. Gordon Tullock is alive and well, and still teeming with original ideas.

References

Becker, G. S. (1976), *The Economic Approach to Human Behavior*, Chicago: University of Chicago Press.

Black, D. (1948), 'On the rationale of group decision-making', *Journal of Political Economy*, LVI: 23–34.

Brady, G. L., and R. D. Tollison (1991), 'Gordon Tullock: creative maverick of public choice', *Public Choice*, 71(3): 141–8.

Buchanan, J. M. (1987), 'The qualities of a natural economist', in C. K. Rowley (ed.), *Democracy and Public Choice: Essays in Honor of Gordon Tullock*, Oxford and New York: Blackwell, pp. 9–19.

Buchanan, J. M., and G. Tullock (1962), *The Calculus of Consent: Logical Foundations of Constitutional Democracy*, Ann Arbor: University of Michigan Press.

Downs, A. (1957), *An Economic Theory of Democracy*, New York: Harper & Row.

Parkinson, C. N. (1957), *Parkinson's Law*, New York: Houghton Mifflin.

Popper, K. (1959), *The Logic of Scientific Discovery*, New York: Basic Books.

Reder, M. W. (1982), 'Chicago economics: permanence and change', *Journal of Economic Literature*, 20: 1–38.

Rowley, C. K. (1987), 'Natural economist or Popperian logician?', in C. K. Rowley (ed.), *Democracy and Public Choice: Essays in Honor of Gordon Tullock*, Oxford and New York: Blackwell, pp. 20–26.

Rowley, C. K. (1991), 'Gordon Tullock: entrepreneur of public choice', *Public Choice*, 71(3): 149–70.

Rowley, C. K. (1993), *The Right to Justice*, Aldershot and Brookfield, VT: Edward Elgar.

Rowley, C. K. (1996), 'The Virginia School of political economy', in F. Foldvary (ed.), *Beyond Neoclassical Economics: Heterodox Approaches to Economic Theory*, Cheltenham and Brookfield, VT: Edward Elgar.

Rowley, C.K. (1999), 'Five market-friendly Nobelists: Friedman, Stigler, Buchanan, Coase and Becker', *Independent Review: A Journal of Political Economy*, III: 413–31.

Rowley, C. K. (2003), 'Gordon Tullock at four score years: an evaluation', in C. K. Rowley and F. Schneider (eds), *The Encyclopedia of Public Choice*, vol. 1, Dordrecht, Boston, MA, and London: Kluwer Academic Publishers, pp. 105–17.

Rowley, C.K. (2005), 'Gordon Tullock: the man and his scholarship', *Public Choice*, 122(1–2): 1–8.

Rowley, C. K., and M. A. Vachris (1995), 'Why democracy does not necessarily produce efficient results', *Journal of Public Choice and Public Finance*, 10: 97–111.

Rowley, C. K., and M. A. Vachris (2003), 'Efficiency of democracy?', in C. K. Rowley and F. Schneider (eds), *The Encyclopedia of Public Choice*, vol. 2, Dordrecht, Boston, MA, and London: Kluwer Academic Publishers, pp. 189–94.

Schumpeter, J. A. (1942), *Capitalism and Democracy*, New York: Harper & Row.

Stigler, G. J., and G. S. Becker (1977) 'De gustibus non est disputandum', *American Economic Review*, 67: 76–90.

Tollison, R. D. (1989), 'Chicago political economy', *Public Choice*, 63: 293–8.

Tollison, R. D. (2003), 'Chicago political economy', in C. K. Rowley and F. Schneider (eds), *The Encyclopedia of Public Choice*, vol. 2, pp. 74–5.

Tullock, G. (1959), 'Problems of majority voting', *Journal of Political Economy*, 67: 571–9.

Tullock, G. (1961a), 'An economic analysis of political choice', *Il Politico*, 16: 234–40.

Tullock, G. (1961b), 'Utility, strategy and social decision rules: comment', *Quarterly Journal of Economics*, 75: 493–7.

Tullock, G. (1965), *The Politics of Bureaucracy*, Washington, DC: Public Affairs Press.

Tullock, G. (1966), *The Organization of Inquiry*, Durham: Duke University Press.

Tullock, G. (1967), *Toward a Mathematics of Politics*, Ann Arbor: University of Michigan Press.

Tullock, G. (1976), *The Vote Motive*, Hobart Paperback 9, London: Institute of Economic Affairs.

Tullock G. (2004), *Virginia Political Economy*, vol. 1 of *The Selected Works of Gordon Tullock* (ed. and with an introduction by C. K. Rowley), Indianapolis, IN: Liberty Fund.

Tullock, G. (with J. M. Buchanan) ([1962] 2004), *The Calculus of Consent: Logical Foundations of Constitutional Democracy*, vol. 2 of *The Selected Works of Gordon Tullock* (ed. and with an introduction by C. K. Rowley), Indianapolis, IN: Liberty Fund.

Tullock, G. ([1966] 2004), *The Organization of Inquiry*, vol. 3 of *The Selected Works of Gordon Tullock* (ed. and with an introduction by C. K. Rowley), Indianapolis, IN: Liberty Fund.

Tullock, G. (2005a), *The Economics of Politics*, vol. 4 of *The Selected Works of Gordon Tullock* (ed. and with an introduction by C. K. Rowley), Indianapolis, IN: Liberty Fund.

Tullock, G. (2005b), *The Rent-Seeking Society*, vol. 5 of *The Selected Works of Gordon Tullock* (ed. and with an introduction by C. K. Rowley), Indianapolis, IN: Liberty Fund.

Tullock, G. (2005c) *Bureaucracy*, vol. 6 of *The Selected Works of Gordon Tullock* (ed. and with an introduction by C. K. Rowley), Indianapolis, IN: Liberty Fund.

Tullock, G. (2005d), *The Economics and Politics of Wealth Redistribution*, vol. 7 of *The Selected Works of Gordon Tullock* (ed. and with an introduction by C. K. Rowley), Indianapolis, IN: Liberty Fund.

Tullock, G. (2005e), *The Social Dilemma: Of Autocracy, Revolution, Coup d'Etat and War*, vol. 8 of *The Selected Works of Gordon Tullock* (ed. and with an introduction by C. K. Rowley), Indianapolis, IN: Liberty Fund.

Tullock, G. (2005f), *Law and Economics*, vol. 9 of *The Selected Works of Gordon Tullock* (ed. and with an introduction by C. K. Rowley), Indianapolis, IN: Liberty Fund.

Tullock, G. (2006), *Economics without Frontiers*, vol. 10 of *The Selected Works of Gordon Tullock* (ed. and with an introduction by C. K. Rowley), Indianapolis, IN: Liberty Fund.

2 THIRTY YEARS ON: TULLOCK, *THE VOTE MOTIVE* AND PUBLIC CHOICE

Stefan Voigt, University of Kassel and ICER, Turin

'Gordon votes'

(Graffito in the men's toilet of the Center for Study of Public Choice when Tullock was still teaching there.)

Prelude

It is quite unusual that a survey, or rather, as Gordon Tullock himself describes his 1976 paper (p. 94), a presentation of 'a few simple, but fundamental, examples', gets reprinted 30 years later. This is especially so since a number of excellent up-to-date surveys are around, such as Dennis Mueller's *Public Choice III* (2003), which contains more than 750 pages. So why bother to turn to a paper that is 30 years old?

A very simple answer could be: because the examples chosen by Tullock 30 years ago still constitute the core of public choice today. Another simple answer could be: because Tullock anticipated a number of results that were rigorously proven only some time after his paper had appeared. Yet another answer could be: because Tullock loves to talk straight – and in this paper one can almost hear him talk. All these answers are valid. Yet my own answer to the question would be: because the application of economics to politics, or simply, public choice, has turned out to be such a huge success since the paper first appeared 30 years ago, and Tullock was instrumental in that success.

In his introduction to the 1976 paper, Arthur Seldon points out that the paper is a 'virtually new subject' (p. ix) for British economic teaching, political debate and press discussion. It is hard to believe that this was written only 30 years ago. In the meantime, no serious economics faculty could do without at least an introductory course in public choice. This is not true only for British universities but would hold for most continental European countries. It is worth turning to the paper again because this development would almost certainly not have been as fast and sweeping had Gordon Tullock not been so enthusiastic in convincing others of the advantages of the then still relatively young research programme. Tullock was not only decisive for the creation and development of the research programme of public choice, but also for *Public Choice*, the journal, as well as for Public Choice, the learned society that meets once a year and is a forum for the discussion of new results within the research programme.

It is no exaggeration to call Tullock 'the entrepreneur of public choice'. Most scholarly journals would publish one volume each (calendar) year. Not so *Public Choice*: there are four new volumes each year, which explains why at the time of writing these lines *Public Choice* had just finished its volume 125. By now, the European Public Choice Society is firmly established and its annual meetings are attended by some two to three hundred scholars. Gordon Tullock has missed only very few of these meetings. He spends lots of time in Europe and does not get tired of giving introductory lectures on public choice. Similar versions were also translated into French and Spanish.

The remainder of these remarks are structured as follows: the following section highlights some important insights of the 1976 paper, while the third section describes the development of the public choice programme over the last 30 years with a special emphasis on Europe. The fourth section deals with a couple of points that seem to be worth quarrelling with, and the final section speculates about the possible future development of public choice.

Impact and insights of the paper

Early in 2006, the academic search engine 'www.scholar.google.com' came up with 32 citations of the 1976 paper. The French and the Spanish version did not do that well but were also quoted ten times. This search engine counts only citations that have left some traces on the Web, which means that the bulk of citations of older papers are not counted at all. One could, hence, presume that the paper has been quoted quite a bit and – probably even more noteworthy – is still quoted to this very day. There is thus some reason to call it 'a classic'. Yet this way of approaching the impact of the paper probably underestimates its importance: for many, this paper – and others also published by the Institute of Economic Affairs in the 1970s – was their first encounter with public choice theory. Most probably, some of its readers decided to dig deeper into the emerging field and make contributions of their own. This is, however, unlikely to show up in the citations, as one would rarely cite an introductory essay.

The 'few simple, but fundamental examples' that Tullock chose for his paper still belong to the core of public choice 30 years on. No textbook on the topic could do without the median voter theorem, without the differences between first past the vote and proportional representation, without logrolling, or the economic theory of bureaucracy. No textbook could do without confronting so-called market failure with government failure and pointing out that we have to make choices between implementable alternatives – and should not compare textbook dreams with the cumbersome real world. This necessity is still being dealt with in academic treatises (see, for example, Dixit, 1996, or the concept of 'remediableness' introduced by Williamson, 1996).

During the development of public choice, Gordon Tullock was frequently the first to deal with a new topic. The economic theory of bureaucracy is only one example of that. Today, Niskanen's book (1971) is supposedly the most cited treatise on the topic, yet Tullock's monograph had appeared already in 1965. The way in which he makes the reader familiar with the basics of this theory is still worthy of being read today. Not only does he explain in plain words why the bureaucracy would tend to offer a quantity of the bureaucratic services that exceeds the socially optimal amount. In addition, he observes that the bureaucrat's preference for leisure turns out, at least to a degree, to be a blessing for society. Observing an ironic twist also seems typical of his work.

The way Tullock deals with the possible pitfalls of logrolling and potential remedies for its welfare-reducing effects is an example of another of his characteristics: he seems to be quite audacious in his recommendations. In order to reduce the likelihood of welfare-reducing logrolling he recommends a two-thirds majority rule. It was shown only later on (Caplin and Nalebuff, 1988) that the 64 per cent majority rule has a number of desirable characteristics, such as being proof against the problem of 'cycling' over the alternatives (a problem that Tullock has dealt with again and again over his long career). Audacity combined with a great intuition of the underlying mechanisms has been a core trait of Tullock's.

The development of public choice over the last 30 years

At the beginning of his paper, Tullock remarks that there has been relatively little empirical testing of the new theory. This has, of course, dramatically changed over the last 30 years. Indeed, the majority of the contributions to *Public Choice*, the journal, seem to have at least an empirical part. But this is not the only way in which the research programme has evolved over the last three decades.

Since most of the founding fathers of the research programme originated in the USA, it seemed only natural that their interest in understanding and explaining politics was equivalent to understanding and explaining *democratic* politics. After all, the USA had been a democratic state for some two hundred years already. Yet collective decision-making in most societies during most of history was not structured according to democratic rules but took place rather autocratically. If the method of rational choice was as universal as its adherents claimed, its application to non-democratic decision-making should still enable us to gain new insights into the working of non-democratic regimes. Here again,

Tullock was among the pioneers (1974, 1987). In the meantime, the topic has not only been picked up by fellow students of public choice such as Wintrobe (1998) or Olson (1991), but the question concerning the economic performance of autocracies has been dealt with by a broad variety of scholars lately (Mulligan et al., 2004).

The next logical step after having dealt with the functioning of democracy on the one hand and the functioning of autocracy on the other would seem to be to deal with transitions from one mode of collective decision-making to the other. This would almost seem to suggest itself in a post-1990 world. Yet few public choice scholars have dealt with the issue yet. But the topic is being picked up by other economists, such as Acemoglu and Robinson (2001).

When Tullock wrote his paper, he pointed out that about half of the presidents of the Public Choice Society had been economists and the other half political scientists. In the meantime, the rational choice approach applied to politics has 'infected' representatives of other disciplines such as legal scholars. The programme has become so broad that various 'sub-programmes' have emerged: a group of public choice scholars is, for example, primarily interested in both the legitimacy of state action and understanding the effects of basic – i.e. constitutional – rules. This research programme is called constitutional political economy and can be traced back to Buchanan and Tullock's *Calculus of Consent* (1962). Representatives of this programme also have their own journal (*Constitutional Political Economy*), which is already in its seventeenth year. As this programme is also interested in very fundamental normative questions, it has bridged the gap to philosophers. This has also helped in setting up new programmes in Politics, Philosophy and Economics in various British and US universities which try to overcome the division between the three disciplines and aim, instead, at a more unified approach.

The output produced is so large that there are a number of additional journals whose content is based on public choice. In Europe, the *European Journal of Political Economy* needs to be mentioned first. But there are a number of other journals around that also carry primarily public-choice-related work. The *Journal of Public Finance and Public Choice*, a journal edited in Italy, is just one such example. Actually, one could even ask to what extent specialised journals are necessary any more: public choice thinking has become part of the mainstream and it is hard to find any issue of more general journals like the *American Economic Review*, the *Quarterly Journal of Economics* or the *Economic Journal* that does not carry papers which pay explicit attention to issues of political economy that used to be marginal only 30 years ago.

The success of the programme seems to have been so sweeping that even brilliant scholars have problems in acknowledging their intellectual ancestors. In their highly acclaimed book *The Economic Effects of Constitutions*, Persson and Tabellini (2003: 5) refer to public choice/constitutional political economy in a footnote and write: '… But this literature is mostly normative and has not led to a careful empirical analysis of the economic effects of alternative constitutional features, with the main exception of a few interesting papers on referenda.' I suspect that one of the reasons why Persson and Tabellini might have problems in identifying with public choice could be that some of those belonging to 'Virginia Political Economy' – Tullock among them – are seen as a rather conservative group. If there is a difference between US and European public choice scholars, it could be that – at least on average – the Americans are indeed more conservative than their European counterparts.

Some quarrels with the paper – and public choice in general

I am fairly sure that Gordon would find these lines rather dull if they only contained praise of his work but did not try to quarrel at least with some issues dealt with in the paper. This section contains, hence, a number of points that could be identified as weak points of the paper, but that have also been weak points of the entire programme.

It is well known that if people vote out of the concern to elect a government that suits their own preferences best, it is hard to explain why people vote at all. In most societies beyond a certain size, the likelihood of casting the decisive vote is, for practical purposes, so close to zero that it is basically zero. Now, if showing up at the ballot box and casting a vote there is not fun in and of itself but is rather costly, then, again, it is hard to explain why people bother to vote. This problem was identified quite early by public choice scholars and dozens of papers have dealt with it. Again, Tullock (1967) had an early contribution to the debate, advancing the argument that the act of voting itself would confer additional utility on to the person voting. Nevertheless, there seems to be consensus among public choice scholars that 'the vote motive' (the title of Tullock's paper at any rate) is still the largest unresolved question of the entire research programme (see, for example, Shughart and Tollison, 2005: 3). It is, hence, somewhat of a puzzle why Tullock chose *The Vote Motive* as a title, as he barely deals with the issue in the paper.[1]

It was just mentioned that some of today's best political economy scholars have problems in acknowledging their public choice ancestors. Well, a similar reproach could also be held against Tullock himself when he writes (p. 36) that 'It is unfortunate but true that the economic approach to politics raises ethical issues.' Why would it be unfortunate? Tullock does advance a reason ('because we are not likely in the near future to reach general agreement on the morality of ... '), which does not convince me. Economics as a discipline emerged out of moral philosophy. Adam Smith, the forefather of the discipline, was both a philosopher and an economist. One could now argue that leaning too much towards the philosophical side would inhibit further progress on the positive side or that owing to the necessity of increased specialisation, nobody could master both the positive and the normative, but that is not the argument Tullock advances. He simply points out the low likelihood of reaching agreement. This does not convince me since we have to make moral choices all the time, even if there is only a low likelihood of consent. The year before Tullock's paper appeared, Buchanan

---

1   The graffito cited at the beginning of this contribution highlights another trait often attributed to Tullock: he lives what he teaches.

had published his *The Limits of Liberty* (1975). Buchanan's book can be read as a masterly treatment of exactly this issue: how should societies coordinate their interactions given that there is a low likelihood of consent on substantive issues? How can societies peacefully live together given that everlasting metaphysical truths are not on offer in modern societies any more?

This unconvincing treatment concerning the relationship between positive and normative analysis leads directly to a methodological issue – and often further to a methodological inconsistency. Public choice scholars start from the premise that in predicting human behaviour it makes sense to assume that human beings behave as if they were maximising their individual utility functions. This would hold not only with regard to business interactions but the assumption could be meaningfully applied in all walks of life: in family interactions, in religious behaviour and – obviously – with regard to collective decision-making, i.e. politics. And indeed, many hypotheses based on these assumptions could not be refuted; our knowledge concerning the functioning of politics has greatly increased and the benevolent dictator (the God of many neoclassical economists) is all but dead. But the research programme, in order to remain consistent, must assume that *all* actors behave as if they were maximising their individual utility functions. This includes academic observers of collective decision-making. Two questions immediately come to the fore: (1) Is there any role for normative advice at all? (2) If there is, who has incentives to give 'good' advice, supposedly advice that increases societal welfare, whatever that could be?

The first question is obviously a substantial question for think tanks like the Institute of Economic Affairs. From a – somewhat extreme – public choice point of view, one can argue that there is no role for advice at all. If all actors behave as if they maximised their individual utility function, why would anybody change her behaviour simply because someone else advised her to do so? Why should an 'advisee' trust an adviser to be interested in improving her utility – instead of his own (the principal-agent problem)? As soon as one drops the assumption that all actors are perfectly informed, a role for advice opens up – if there is some way to deal with the principal-agent problem. Since perfect information is a very extreme assumption, dropping it does not come at a high cost and there is some role for normative advice even in the world of public choice. In his paper, Tullock describes the self-serving behaviour of the bureaucracy and asks (p. 72) 'What can be done?' He is obviously interested in improvement and discusses various possibilities of competition within bureaus, between bureaus and even between bureaus and private firms. Few of his recommendations have, however, been implemented in the meantime. Why? Because if they make the concerned actors worse off they have few incentives to implement such suggestions – as public choice would predict. Public choice scholars who take their own theory seriously should, hence, only offer advice that is enlightened in the terms of their own theory; in other words: advice ought to keep in mind that the concerned actors only have incentives to implement advice if it does not make them worse off.

The second question is a bit more tricky. What reasons do we have to assume that Tullock – and any other public choice scholar – is interested in increasing the common good if the core assumption of public choice is that all actors – i.e. academics too – are basically driven by their self-interest? One could venture the hypothesis that the reputation mechanism among academics works such that only those scholars who advance the common good in their work enjoy a high degree of reputation within the profession. Advancing such advice would therefore increase one's reputation – and be in line with self-interest. Then again, at least in continental Europe, there seems to exist a fairly strong divide between economists who are strong as academic economists and those who have a good reputation as policy advisers. These two camps seem to treat each other with (more or less) benign neglect and to talk of 'the profession' does not reflect reality. This is, hence, not a convincing way out of the possible impasse. But if there is no convincing answer to this question, the first question (concerning the potential role of normative advice) becomes relevant again. If there are no good reasons to assume that anybody can be trusted in putting forth advice whose implementation would lead to welfare improvements, what is the role of advice? Supposedly, many readers would trust that the suggestions made by Tullock – and many other scholars – would indeed improve the welfare of all. Yet what we need is a systematic argument – and not (only) some kind of trust. As soon as we explicitly introduce the possibility that some actors might indeed be interested in the common good, we should, simply to remain consistent, also introduce the possibility that bureaucrats, ministers, presidents, legislators and so forth can also be interested in the common good. Then again, we would need to specify the conditions under which this seems to be more likely and those under which it seems to be less likely. These issues cannot be dealt with here in any meaningful detail. I will, however, return to them in the concluding section.

A third – and somewhat less basic – point on which I would like to quarrel with Tullock is his position on the desired relationship between the bureaucracy and elected officials. He writes (p. 62): 'Indeed there seems now to be developing a mystique under which the bureaucrats are not even supposed to be under the control of elected officials.' Tullock certainly does not seem to approve of this 'mystique', and explicitly refers to 'that oldest branch of the bureaucracy, the judiciary'. This could be an issue in which the discipline has developed over the last 30 years and Tullock did not anticipate this development (as he did in so many other areas; see above). By now there seems to be widespread consensus that independent central banks – i.e. a bureaucracy explicitly *not* directly accountable to elected officials – lead to lower inflation rates (Berger et al., 2001, is a survey). But the beneficial effects of the bureaucrats not under the control of elected officials are not confined to independent central banks. It has been shown that countries in which prosecutors act independently from the minister of justice and, more generally, from elected officials have lower corruption levels than countries in which the executive has direct control (Voigt et al., 2005). It has also been shown that privatised network industries (such as telecommunications, but also energy) display greater degrees of both innovation and investment, and hence create more consumer welfare, if the bureaus regulating their behaviour are not under the direct control of elected officials (Gual and Trillas, 2004).

Tullock even named the judiciary as part of the bureaucracy. This is a rather unorthodox classification of the judiciary. Here, I do not want to quarrel with that classification but rather with the issue of the effects of judiciaries that are not under the control of elected officials. A state that is powerful enough to enforce private property systematically faces a difficult problem: since it is so powerful, the promises of its representatives to factually enforce private property rights are not very credible as long as representatives of the state can make themselves better off by promising the enforcement of private property rights and then, once private actors are invested, not honouring their previous promises. If they were able to make credible commitments, everybody could be better off since private actors would invest more and the tax receipts of the state could also be higher. It has been argued (Feld and Voigt, 2003) that an independent judiciary can be interpreted as a tool to turn simple promises into credible commitments. It has been shown (Feld and Voigt, 2004) that factually independent judiciaries are indeed significantly and robustly linked to higher economic growth in a sample of more than seventy countries. The logic here applied to the judiciary can also be applied to bureaus: their independence allows the politicians to turn promises into credible commitments which increase overall welfare. Independent bureaus can thus be interpreted as an important element of a modern notion of separation of powers that helps to achieve results that would be unattainable were these bureaus under the direct control of elected officials.

Possible developments

In the last section, we touched on the issue of adequate behavioural assumptions. We are, of course, not the first to deal with these issues.

One might even say that there is a new development among leading public choice scholars to broaden the traditional behavioural assumptions. Bruno Frey (1997), for example, has argued that a constitution for knaves crowds out civic virtues, implying that the 'worst case behavioural assumptions' are close to a self-fulfilling prophecy. Geoffrey Brennan and Alan Hamlin (2000), to name just two more prominent public choice scholars, make an explicit argument 'beyond *homo oeconomicus*'. Behavioural economics has made great progress over the last couple of years without, however, having been able to define a broader behavioural model that allows for both selfish and non-selfish behaviour. This is, hence, a challenge not only for public choice. But it seems to be especially relevant for public choice as collective decision-making seems to be influenced by a variety of very heterogeneous motivations.

References

Acemoglu, D., and J. Robinson (2001), 'A theory of political transitions', *American Economic Review*, 91(4): 938–63.

Berger, H., J. de Haan and S. Eijffinger (2001), 'Central bank independence: an update of theory and evidence', *Journal of Economic Surveys*, 15: 3–40.

Brennan, G., and A. Hamlin (2000), *Democratic Devices and Desires*, Cambridge: Cambridge University Press.

Buchanan, J. M. (1975), *The Limits of Liberty: Between Anarchy and Leviathan*, Chicago, IL: University of Chicago Press.

Buchanan, J. M., and G. Tullock (1962), *The Calculus of Consent: Logical Foundations of Constitutional Democracy*, Ann Arbor: University of Michigan Press.

Caplin, A., and B. Nalebuff (1988) 'On 64%-majority rule', *Econometrica*, 56: 787–814.

Dixit, A. (1996), *The Making of Economic Policy: A Transaction-Cost Politics Perspective*, Munich Lectures in Economics, Center for Economic Studies, Cambridge: MIT Press.

Feld, L. P., and S. Voigt (2003), 'Economic growth and judicial independence: cross-country evidence using a new set of indicators', *European Journal of Political Economy*, 19(3): 497–527.

Feld, L. P., and S. Voigt (2004), 'Making judges independent: some proposals regarding the judiciary', CESifo Working Paper no. 1260.

Frey, B. (1997), 'A constitution for knaves crowds out civic virtues', *Economic Journal*, 107: 1043–53.

Gual, J., and F. Trillas (2004), 'Telecommunications policies: determinants and impacts', available at http://papers.ssrn.com/sol3/papers.cfm?abstract_id=459220.

Mueller, D. (2003), *Public Choice III*, Cambridge: Cambridge University Press.

Mulligan, C. B., R. Gil and X. Sala-i-Martin (2004), 'Do democracies have different public policies than nondemocracies?', *Journal of Economic Perspectives*, 18(1): 51–74.

Niskanen, W. (1971), *Bureaucracy and Representative Government*, Chicago, IL: Aldine-Atherton.

Olson, M. (1991), 'Autocracy, democracy, and prosperity', in R. Zeckhauser (ed.), *Strategy and Choice*, Cambridge, MA: MIT Press, pp. 131–57.

Persson, T., and G. Tabellini (2003), *The Economic Effects of Constitutions*, Cambridge, MA: MIT Press.

Shughart, W. F., and R. Tollison (2005), 'Public choice in the new century', *Public Choice*, 124(1–2): 1–18.

Tullock, G. (1965), *The Politics of Bureaucracy*, Washington, DC: Public Affairs Press.

Tullock, G. (1967), *Toward a Mathematics of Politics*, Ann Arbor: University of Michigan Press.

Tullock, G. (1974), *The Social Dilemma: The Economics of War and Revolution*, Blacksburg: Center for Study of Public Choice.

Tullock, G. (1976), *The Vote Motive*, Hobart Paperback 9, London: Institute of Economic Affairs.

Tullock, G. (1987), *Autocracy*, Dordrecht: Kluwer Academic Publishers.

Voigt, S., L. Feld and A. v. Aaken (2005), 'Power over prosecutors corrupts politicians: cross country evidence using a new indicator', paper presented at the Annual Meeting of the Public Choice Society, March, New Orleans, available at http://www.pubchoicesoc.org/papers2005/Voigt_Feld_van_Aaken.pdf.

Williamson, O. (1996), *The Mechanisms of Governance*, Oxford: Oxford University Press.

Wintrobe, R. (1998), *The Political Economy of Dictatorship*, Cambridge: Cambridge University Press.

3   A RETROSPECTIVE ASSESSMENT OF TULLOCK'S *THE VOTE MOTIVE*

Michael C. Munger, Duke University

Characteristically, however, the overthrow of the dictator simply means that there will be another dictator. ... the policies they follow will probably not be radically different. If we look around the world, we quickly realize that these policies will not be radically different from those that would be followed by a democracy either. (Tullock, 1987: 20)

Some retrospective perspective

The tradition of government action and regulation in economics is founded in the doctrine of market failure. More specifically, government action is justified as follows: *Decentralised market processes fail to achieve Pareto efficient results in the case of {blank}, so government action is required.* This claim is taken to be sufficient (though hardly necessary) as an authoritative argument. And, as any student of modern economics knows, the {blank} can be filled in with some combination of (a) information asymmetry, (b) natural monopoly, (c) externalities or public goods, or (d) inequity in wealth distribution.

Proponents of this view do not consider it to be inherently negative, or pessimistic. The results of the market failure approach simply demonstrate the inefficiency of pure market processes with reference to a benchmark where information, coordination and agency costs are negligible.

The public choice view disagrees with, or at a minimum does not concede the sufficiency of, the 'market failure implies government makes things better' argument. This counterpoint is argued effectively in many places, but it was argued perhaps most succinctly, and most comprehensively, in Tullock's *The Vote Motive* (1976). More than a few current public choice scholars first encountered their now-favoured line of reasoning in this slender volume. It is important to recognise that Tullock's 'government failure' view is no more pessimistic, and no more inherently ideological, than the market failure view. Tullock's genius was to answer the market failures argument by applying similarly well-defined and positive benchmarks to the likely performance of democratic or bureaucratic institutions.

By the time *The Vote Motive* was published, there was a flourishing tradition of public choice scholarship, of course. In political science, my own (adopted) discipline, it has been argued that the 'Pentateuch' of public choice was (in chronological order) Arrow (1951); Downs (1957); Black (1958); Buchanan and Tullock (1962); and Olson (1965), followed closely within political science in particular by Riker (1962), Rae (1967) and Farquharson (1969).[1] Furthermore, by the time *The Vote Motive* was published, there were vigorous and various perspectives in journals ranging from the *American Political Science Review* to the *American Economic Review* to journals in Europe and Asia.[2]

Nonetheless, *The Vote Motive* made a remarkable contribution to the expansion of the scope of public choice as a social science approach. In fact, Tullock proved prescient in several ways in this book, not least when he says, 'Today it is not possible to tell whether the author of an article using economic tools in political science was originally an economist or a political scientist' (p. 35). Indeed. Today, 30 years later, the very ideas of 'economic tools' rings hollow, because the use of rational choice approaches and models is one of the dominant paradigms. As Pion-Berlin and Cleary (2005) lament, more than one fifth of all papers in the *American Political Science Review* now use something very close to public choice modelling. In modern political science, to paraphrase

---

1   The 'Public Choice Pentateuch' is due to Grofman (2004). His second tier of influential public choice books includes the other three listed here.
2   The most comprehensive review of the public choice literature in all its forms is Mueller (2003).

Milton Friedman, 'We are all public choice theorists now.'[3]

One reason for the success of Tullock's efforts is the economy and elegance of the taxonomy of government failures he offers in *The Vote Motive*. For the sake of simplicity and brevity, I will summarise these as follows:

I The failure of forbearance

We cannot rely on government, or governors, to restrain themselves. All actors in the public sphere, from voters to bureaucrats to elected officials to dictators, act in their self-interest. Theories that fail to take this into account rest on a confusion between what people say and what they do, according to Tullock. One cannot help taking a perverse satisfaction in the accuracy of Tullock's observations in this regard. We are constantly confronted with the implications of assuming forbearance: a politician tells us what we want to hear, and then does something else. The only thing that should mystify us at this point is that we are still *surprised* at the failure of forbearance as a mechanism of control.

II Information elicitation and preference revelation

One of the key features of markets is the generation of information about relative scarcity through prices. Perfectly competitive markets produce perfectly accurate information, but even badly distorted markets produce a lot of usable information. Government attempts to 'correct' for externalities through a system of Pigouvian taxes and subsidies are flying blind. Such attempts are likely to be (at best) misguided and inaccurate, or (at worst) blatantly opportunistic and exploitative. Tullock suggests, based on his own research on the preference revelation problem (Tideman and Tullock, 1976), that this problem makes

---

3   Though one should be careful with Friedman's attributed 'We are all Keynesians now'. As Friedman (1968) said, giving the context for the claim: 'We all use the Keynesian language and apparatus, none of us any longer accepts the initial Keynesian conclusions.'

government no more, and probably less, competent to regulate extern-alities at the (unobservable) socially optimum level.[4]

III Bureaucrats are like other men

In Chapter 4 of the book, Tullock synthesises the work of a variety of previous scholars in a remarkably short space. He rightly credits Niskanen (1971) with having broken much of this ground, but Tullock did more than just summarise. The idea that 'bureaucrats are like other men' is very powerful, because it means that the internal workings of government agencies can be subjected to the particular brand of economic analysis that was to become the hallmark of public choice. Tullock anticipates much of the 'agency theory' applied to bureaucra-cies in later decades,[5] as well as raising a number of interesting research questions on competition among and within bureaus which have yet to be answered.

IV Why so much stability?

Though Tullock did not ask his famous question in *The Vote Motive*, he clearly lays the groundwork for his later contributions (Tullock, 1981) and those who changed the discipline of political science as a result (for example, Shepsle and Weingast, 1981).

What 'why so much stability?' means is this: our models predict

---

4   My friend William Dougan, of Clemson University, made a remarkably simple but sig-nificant connection over coffee one cold autumn day at a shop on campus at the Uni-versity of Chicago, where we happened both to be visiting. The observation is this: the Coase problem (Coase, 1960), where externalities are internalised by market processes if not prevented from doing so by transactions costs, is actually closely related to Hayek's 'knowledge problem' (Hayek, 1945). Markets are the lowest-cost producer of information about how externalities are valued. Hayek's objection to government organisation of pro-duction applies with at least equal force to generating information about externalities, and perhaps more so. It was like a lot of really important and useful observations: obvi-ous, when you think about it.

5   See, for example, Weingast (1984).

constant turnover in political decisions, because of the non-existence of a Condorcet winner for most arbitrarily chosen configurations of preferences in any political context of dimension 2 or higher. Presumably, that should mean that there is consistent, cycling change in policy, and that no incumbent should survive more than one term. In actual politics, however, we observe nearly the opposite. Far from entropic variation, or even cycles, we observe stability, and incumbency advantage approaching invulnerability. The re-election rate in the US House of Representatives, for example, is more than 90 per cent.

The Vote Motive, of course, was published five years before the 1981 *Public Choice* paper on 'Why So Much Stability?' We can see clear antecedents, however, particularly in his discussion of logrolling, for the later path-breaking work in political science. Tullock offers an insightful and dispassionate analysis of the values and defects of logrolling in a political system. This expression of the nature of the exchange basis of government institutions, in striking analogy to the exchange basis of market institutions, has held up very well. I was struck by how re-reading it, even 30 years later, would still help most students and faculty understand the pressures of day-to-day politics on parties, leaders and coalitions.

Some even more retrospective perspective

One of the most striking things about the public choice perspective in political science is its self-conscious linkages to political theory and political philosophy. In the last brief chapter, Tullock outlines once again his purpose in writing the book, and in writing it in this particular way, focusing on what he called 'fundamental examples'.

There is something I have found striking, in the twenty years since I myself converted to political science (having been catechised as an economist, but soon revealed to be in a number of ways wallowing in apostasy). And that is the way in which the public choice perspective embodied in Gordon's prolegomenon, *The Vote Motive*, holds up not just looking forward, but looking *backwards*. That is, the public choice perspective reveals and uncovers truths about the nature of collective choice in classic literature also. In closing, then, let me give two examples of how well public choice theory can predict, not just the future, but the past. The first is Plutarch's account of the *ostracism*, or banishment, of Aristides about 480 BCE through a collective choice process.

> It was performed, to be short, in this manner. Every one taking an
> *ostracon*, a sherd, that is, or piece of earthenware, wrote upon it the
> citizen's name he would have banished, and carried it to a certain
> part of the marketplace surrounded with wooden rails. First, the
> magistrates numbered all the sherds in gross (for if there were less
> than six thousand, the ostracism was imperfect); then, laying every
> name by itself, they pronounced him whose name was written by
> the larger number, banished for ten years, with the enjoyment of
> his estate. As, therefore, they were writing the names on the sherds,
> it is reported that an illiterate clownish fellow, giving Aristides
> his sherd, supposing him a common citizen, begged him to write
> *Aristides* upon it; and he being surprised and asking if Aristides
> had ever done him any injury, 'None at all', said he, 'neither know I
> the man; but I am tired of hearing him everywhere called the Just'.
> Aristides, hearing this, is said to have made no reply, but returned
> the sherd with his own name inscribed. At his departure from the
> city, lifting up his hands to heaven, he made a prayer, (the reverse,
> it would seem, of that of Achilles), that the Athenians might never
> have any occasion which should constrain them to remember
> Aristides. (Plutarch, 1517: 396)

Notice that Plutarch's story has people acting in what they think might be their self-interest, but that this self-interest is narrow and petty and ignorant, grist for the Tullockian mill. In addition, we see that the institutions, or the way votes are counted, can determine the outcome. Ostracism used the simplest form of plurality rule; whoever got the most votes lost, and had to leave the city in disgrace. As public choice theorists know well, of course, plurality decision rules have unattractive properties, but they are definitely decisive.

The second example is the description of the state of leadership in democracy given by Polybius about 130 BCE:

> The Athenian [democracy] is always in the position of a ship
> without a commander. In such a ship, if fear of the enemy, or the
> occurrence of a storm induce the crew to be of one mind and to
> obey the helmsman, everything goes well; but if they recover from
> this fear, and begin to treat their officers with contempt, and to
> quarrel with each other because they are no longer all of one mind
> – one party wishing to continue the voyage, and the other urging
> the steersman to bring the ship to anchor; some letting out the
> sheets, and others hauling them in, and ordering the sails to be
> furled – their discord and quarrels make a sorry show to lookers
> on; and the position of affairs is full of risk to those on board
> engaged on the same voyage; and the result has often been that,
> after escaping the dangers of the widest seas, and the most violent
> storms, they wreck their ship in harbour, and close to shore.
> (Polybius, 1889: ch. 44)

This sounds to me like the sort of example that those who claim great things for government often invoke against Tullock's 'bureaucrats are like other men' claim. It is true that military units are among the most bureaucratic and hidebound of organisations. And it is also true that military units sometimes (though not always) represent the highest ideals of patriotism, and achieve heroic feats without the benefit of market incentives. But it is chimerical to reason about bureaucracies from their few, isolated successes. Who cannot sympathise with Polybius's biting observation that democracies, 'after escaping the dangers of the widest seas, and the most violent storms … wreck their ship in harbour, and close to shore'?

As a final observation, I offer a quote from H. L. Mencken. I have no way of knowing, of course, what Mencken would have thought of *The Vote Motive*. But I suspect he would have nodded grimly at several of the sections concerned with positive theory, suspicions Mencken harboured from experience:

> It [is impossible] to separate the democratic idea from the
> theory that there is a mystical merit, an esoteric and ineradicable
> rectitude, in the man at the bottom of the scale – that inferiority,

by some strange magic, becomes superiority – nay, the superiority of superiorities. … What baffles statesmen is to be solved by the people, instantly and by a sort of seraphic intuition. … This notion, as I hint, originated in the poetic fancy of gentlemen on the upper levels – sentimentalists who, observing to their distress that the ass was overladen, proposed to reform transportation by putting him in the cart. (Mencken, 1926: 3–4)

References

Arrow, K. ([1951] 1962), *Social Choice and Individual Values*, New York: Wiley.

Black, D. (1958), *The Theory of Committees and Elections*, London and New York: Cambridge University Press.

Buchanan, J. M., and G. Tullock (1962), *The Calculus of Consent: Logical Foundations of Constitutional Democracy*, Ann Arbor: University of Michigan Press.

Coase, R. H. (1960), 'The problem of social cost', *Journal of Law and Economics*, 3: 1–44.

Downs, A. (1957), *An Economic Theory of Democracy*, New York: Harper & Row.

Farquharson, R. (1969), *Theory of Voting*, New Haven, CT: Yale University Press.

Friedman, M. (1968), 'Why economists disagree', in *Dollars and Deficits: Living with America's Economic Problems*, Englewood Cliffs, NJ: Prentice-Hall, pp. 1–16.

Grofman, B. (2004), 'Reflections on public choice', *Public Choice*, 118: 31–51.

Hayek, F. A. (1945), 'The use of knowledge in society', *American Economic Review*, 35: 519–30.

Mencken, H. L. (1926), *Notes on Democracy*, New York: Knopf.

Mueller, D. C. (2003), *Public Choice III*, New York: Cambridge University Press.

Niskanen, W. (1971), *Bureaucracy and Representative Government*, Chicago, IL: Aldine Atherton.

Olson, M. (1965), *The Logic of Collective Action*, New York: Schocken.

Pion-Berlin, D., and D. Cleary (2005), 'Methodological bias in the *APSR*', in K. Monroe (ed.), *Perestroika!: The Raucous Rebellion in Political Science*, New Haven, CT: Yale University Press.

Plutarch ([1517] 1932), *The Lives of the Noble Grecians and Romans*, trans. J. Dryden, rev. and ed. A. H. Clough, New York: Modern Library.

Polybius (1889), *The Histories of Polybius*, 2 vols, trans. E. S. Shuckburgh, London: Macmillan (original *c.* 130 BCE).

Rae, D. ([1967] 1971), *The Political Consequences of Electoral Laws*, New Haven, CT: Yale University Press.

Riker, W. H. (1962), *The Theory of Political Coalitions*, New Haven, CT: Yale University Press.

Shepsle, K., and B. Weingast (1981), 'Structure-induced equilibrium and legislative choice', *Public Choice*, 37: 503–19.

Tideman, N., and G. Tullock (1976), 'A new and superior process for making social choices', *Journal of Political Economy*, 84: 1145–59.

Tullock, G. (1976), *The Vote Motive*, Hobart Paperback 9, London: Institute of Economic Affairs.

Tullock, G. (1981), 'Why so much stability?', *Public Choice*, 37(2): 189–202.

Tullock, G. (1987), *Autocracy*, Dordrecht: Kluwer Academic Publishers.

Weingast, B. (1984), 'The Congressional-bureaucratic system: a principal agent perspective (with applications to the SEC)', *Public Choice*, 44: 147–91.

ABOUT THE IEA

The Institute is a research and educational charity (No. CC 235 351), limited
by guarantee. Its mission is to improve understanding of the fundamental
institutions of a free society by analysing and expounding the role of market's in
solving economic and social problems.

The IEA achieves its mission by:

- a high-quality publishing programme
- conferences, seminars, lectures and other events
- outreach to school and college students
- brokering media introductions and appearances

The IEA, which was established in 1955 by the late Sir Antony Fisher, is
an educational charity, not a political organisation. It is independent of any
political party or group and does not carry on activities intended to affect
support for any political party or candidate in any election or referendum, or
at any other time. It is financed by sales of publications, conference fees and
voluntary donations.

In addition to its main series of publications the IEA also publishes a
quarterly journal, *Economic Affairs*.

The IEA is aided in its work by a distinguished international Academic
Advisory Council and an eminent panel of Honorary Fellows. Together with
other academics, they review prospective IEA publications, their comments
being passed on anonymously to authors. All IEA papers are therefore subject to
the same rigorous independent refereeing process as used by leading academic
journals.

IEA publications enjoy widespread classroom use and course adoptions
in schools and universities. They are also sold throughout the world and often
translated/reprinted.

Since 1974 the IEA has helped to create a world-wide network of 100
similar institutions in over 70 countries. They are all independent but share the
IEA's mission.

Views expressed in the IEA's publications are those of the authors, not
those of the Institute (which has no corporate view), its Managing Trustees,
Academic Advisory Council members or senior staff.

Members of the Institute's Academic Advisory Council, Honorary Fellows,
Trustees and Staff are listed on the following page.

The Institute gratefully acknowledges financial support for its publications
programme and other work from a generous benefaction by the late Alec and
Beryl Warren.

Other papers recently published by the IEA include:

WHO, What and Why?
Transnational Government, Legitimacy and the World Health Organization
Roger Scruton
Occasional Paper 113; ISBN 0 255 36487 3; £8.00

The World Turned Rightside Up
A New Trading Agenda for the Age of Globalisation
John C. Hulsman
Occasional Paper 114; ISBN 0 255 36495 4; £8.00

The Representation of Business in English Literature
Introduced and edited by Arthur Pollard
Readings 53; ISBN 0 255 36491 1; £12.00

Anti-Liberalism 2000
The Rise of New Millennium Collectivism
David Henderson
Occasional Paper 115; ISBN 0 255 36497 0; £7.50

Capitalism, Morality and Markets
Brian Griffiths, Robert A. Sirico, Norman Barry & Frank Field
Readings 54; ISBN 0 255 36496 2; £7.50

A Conversation with Harris and Seldon
Ralph Harris & Arthur Seldon
Occasional Paper 116; ISBN 0 255 36498 9; £7.50

Malaria and the DDT Story
Richard Tren & Roger Bate
Occasional Paper 117; ISBN 0 255 36499 7; £10.00

A Plea to Economists Who Favour Liberty: Assist the Everyman
Daniel B. Klein
Occasional Paper 118; ISBN 0 255 36501 2; £10.00

The Changing Fortunes of Economic Liberalism
Yesterday, Today and Tomorrow
David Henderson
Occasional Paper 105 (new edition); ISBN 0 255 36520 9; £12.50

The Global Education Industry
Lessons from Private Education in Developing Countries
James Tooley
Hobart Paper 141 (new edition); ISBN 0 255 36503 9; £12.50

Saving Our Streams
The Role of the Anglers' Conservation Association in
Protecting English and Welsh Rivers
Roger Bate
Research Monograph 53; ISBN 0 255 36494 6; £10.00

Better Off Out?
The Benefits or Costs of EU Membership
Brian Hindley & Martin Howe
Occasional Paper 99 (new edition); ISBN 0 255 36502 0; £10.00

Buckingham at 25
Freeing the Universities from State Control
Edited by James Tooley
Readings 55; ISBN 0 255 36512 8; £15.00

Lectures on Regulatory and Competition Policy
Irwin M. Stelzer
Occasional Paper 120; ISBN 0 255 36511 x; £12.50

Misguided Virtue
False Notions of Corporate Social Responsibility
David Henderson
Hobart Paper 142; ISBN 0 255 36510 1; £12.50

HIV and Aids in Schools
The Political Economy of Pressure Groups and Miseducation
Barrie Craven, Pauline Dixon, Gordon Stewart & James Tooley
Occasional Paper 121; ISBN 0 255 36522 5; £10.00

The Road to Serfdom
The Reader's Digest *condensed version*
Friedrich A. Hayek
Occasional Paper 122; ISBN 0 255 36530 6; £7.50

Bastiat's *The Law*
Introduction by Norman Barry
Occasional Paper 123; ISBN 0 255 36509 8; £7.50

A Globalist Manifesto for Public Policy
Charles Calomiris
Occasional Paper 124; ISBN 0 255 36525 x; £7.50

Euthanasia for Death Duties
Putting Inheritance Tax Out of Its Misery
Barry Bracewell-Milnes
Research Monograph 54; ISBN 0 255 36513 6; £10.00

Liberating the Land
The Case for Private Land-use Planning
Mark Pennington
Hobart Paper 143; ISBN 0 255 36508 x; £10.00

IEA Yearbook of Government Performance 2002/2003
Edited by Peter Warburton
Yearbook 1; ISBN 0 255 36532 2; £15.00

Britain's Relative Economic Performance, 1870–1999
Nicholas Crafts
Research Monograph 55; ISBN 0 255 36524 1; £10.00

Should We Have Faith in Central Banks?
Otmar Issing
Occasional Paper 125; ISBN 0 255 36528 4; £7.50

The Dilemma of Democracy
Arthur Seldon
Hobart Paper 136 (reissue); ISBN 0 255 36536 5; £10.00

Capital Controls: a 'Cure' Worse Than the Problem?
Forrest Capie
Research Monograph 56; ISBN 0 255 36506 3; £10.00

The Poverty of 'Development Economics'
Deepak Lal
Hobart Paper 144 (reissue); ISBN 0 255 36519 5; £15.00

Should Britain Join the Euro?
The Chancellor's Five Tests Examined
Patrick Minford
Occasional Paper 126; ISBN 0 255 36527 6; £7.50

Post-Communist Transition: Some Lessons
Leszek Balcerowicz
Occasional Paper 127; ISBN 0 255 36533 0; £7.50

A Tribute to Peter Bauer
John Blundell et al.
Occasional Paper 128; ISBN 0 255 36531 4; £10.00

Employment Tribunals
Their Growth and the Case for Radical Reform
J. R. Shackleton
Hobart Paper 145; ISBN 0 255 36515 2; £10.00

Fifty Economic Fallacies Exposed
Geoffrey E. Wood
Occasional Paper 129; ISBN 0 255 36518 7; £12.50

A Market in Airport Slots
Keith Boyfield (editor), David Starkie, Tom Bass & Barry Humphreys
Readings 56; ISBN 0 255 36505 5; £10.00

Money, Inflation and the Constitutional Position of the Central Bank
Milton Friedman & Charles A. E. Goodhart
Readings 57; ISBN 0 255 36538 1; £10.00

railway.com
Parallels between the Early British Railways and the ICT Revolution
Robert C. B. Miller
Research Monograph 57; ISBN 0 255 36534 9; £12.50

The Regulation of Financial Markets
Edited by Philip Booth & David Currie
Readings 58; ISBN 0 255 36551 9; £12.50

Climate Alarmism Reconsidered
Robert L. Bradley Jr
Hobart Paper 146; ISBN 0 255 36541 1; £12.50

Government Failure: E. G. West on Education
Edited by James Tooley & James Stanfield
Occasional Paper 130; ISBN 0 255 36552 7; £12.50

Waging the War of Ideas
John Blundell
Second edition
Occasional Paper 131; ISBN 0 255 36547 0; £12.50

Corporate Governance: Accountability in the Marketplace
Elaine Sternberg
Second edition
Hobart Paper 147; ISBN 0 255 36542 x; £12.50

The Land Use Planning System
Evaluating Options for Reform
John Corkindale
Hobart Paper 148; ISBN 0 255 36550 0; £10.00

Economy and Virtue
Essays on the Theme of Markets and Morality
Edited by Dennis O'Keeffe
Readings 59; ISBN 0 255 36504 7; £12.50

Free Markets Under Siege
Cartels, Politics and Social Welfare
Richard A. Epstein
Occasional Paper 132; ISBN 0 255 36553 5; £10.00

Unshackling Accountants
D. R. Myddelton
Hobart Paper 149; ISBN 0 255 36559 4; £12.50

The Euro as Politics
Pedro Schwartz
Research Monograph 58; ISBN 0 255 36535 7; £12.50

Pricing Our Roads
Vision and Reality
Stephen Glaister & Daniel J. Graham
Research Monograph 59; ISBN 0 255 36562 4; £10.00

The Role of Business in the Modern World
Progress, Pressures, and Prospects for the Market Economy
David Henderson
Hobart Paper 150; ISBN 0 255 36548 9; £12.50

Public Service Broadcasting Without the BBC?
Alan Peacock
Occasional Paper 133; ISBN 0 255 36565 9; £10.00

The ECB and the Euro: the First Five Years
Otmar Issing
Occasional Paper 134; ISBN 0 255 36555 1; £10.00

Towards a Liberal Utopia?
Edited by Philip Booth
Hobart Paperback 32; ISBN 0 255 36563 2; £15.00

The Way Out of the Pensions Quagmire
Philip Booth & Deborah Cooper
Research Monograph 60; ISBN 0 255 36517 9; £12.50

Black Wednesday
A Re-examination of Britain's Experience in the Exchange Rate Mechanism
Alan Budd
Occasional Paper 135; ISBN 0 255 36566 7; £7.50

Crime: Economic Incentives and Social Networks
Paul Ormerod
Hobart Paper 151; ISBN 0 255 36554 3; £10.00

The Road to Serfdom *with* **The Intellectuals and Socialism**
Friedrich A. Hayek
Occasional Paper 136; ISBN 0 255 36576 4; £10.00

Money and Asset Prices in Boom and Bust
Tim Congdon
Hobart Paper 152; ISBN 0 255 36570 5; £10.00

The Dangers of Bus Re-regulation
and Other Perspectives on Markets in Transport
John Hibbs et al.
Occasional Paper 137; ISBN 0 255 36572 1; £10.00

The New Rural Economy
Change, Dynamism and Government Policy
Berkeley Hill et al.
Occasional Paper 138; ISBN 0 255 36546 2; £15.00

The Benefits of Tax Competition
Richard Teather
Hobart Paper 153; ISBN 0 255 36569 1; £12.50

Wheels of Fortune
Self-funding Infrastructure and the Free Market Case for a Land Tax
Fred Harrison
Hobart Paper 154; ISBN 0 255 36589 6; £12.50

Were 364 Economists All Wrong?
Edited by Philip Booth
Readings 60
ISBN-10: 0 255 36588 8; ISBN-13: 978 0 255 36588 8; £10.00

Europe After the 'No' Votes
Mapping a New Economic Path
Patrick A. Messerlin
Occasional Paper 139
ISBN-10: 0 255 36580 2; ISBN-13: 978 0 255 36580 2; £10.00

The Railways, the Market and the Government
John Hibbs et al.
Readings 61
ISBN-10: 0 255 36567 5; ISBN-13: 978 0 255 36567 3; £12.50

Corruption: The World's Big C
Cases, Causes, Consequences, Cures
Ian Senior
Research Monograph 61
ISBN-10: 0 255 36571 3; ISBN-13: 978 0 255 36571 0; £12.50

Sir Humphrey's Legacy
Facing Up to the Cost of Public Sector Pensions
Neil Record
Hobart Paper 156
ISBN-10: 0 255 36578 0; ISBN-13: 978 0 255 36578 9; £10.00

The Economics of Law
Cento Veljanovski
Second edition
Hobart Paper 157
ISBN-10: 0 255 36561 6; ISBN-13: 978 0 255 36561 1; £12.50

Living with Leviathan
Public Spending, Taxes and Economic Performance
David B. Smith
Hobart Paper 158
ISBN-10: 0 255 36579 9; ISBN-13: 978 0 255 36579 6; £12.50

To order copies of currently available IEA papers, or to enquire about availability, please contact:

Gazelle
IEA orders
FREEPOST RLYS-EAHU-YSCZ
White Cross Mills
Hightown
Lancaster LA1 4XS

Tel: 01524 68765
Fax: 01524 63232
Email: sales@gazellebooks.co.uk

The IEA also offers a subscription service to its publications. For a single annual payment, currently £40.00 in the UK, you will receive every monograph the IEA publishes during the course of a year and discounts on our extensive back catalogue. For more information, please contact:

Adam Myers
Subscriptions
The Institute of Economic Affairs
2 Lord North Street
London SW1P 3LB

Tel: 020 7799 8920
Fax: 020 7799 2137
Website: www.iea.org.uk